# ALL ABOUT

# Portland Head Light

## CAPE ELIZABETH, MAINE

### By Jeremy D'Entremont

CIDER MILL PRESS

BOOK PUBLISHERS
KENNEBUNKPORT, MAINE

13-Digit ISBN: 978-1604337778
10-Digit ISBN: 160433777X

This book may be ordered by mail from the publisher. Please include $5.99 for postage and handling. Please support your local bookseller first!

Books published by Cider Mill Press Book Publishers are available at special discounts for bulk purchases in the United States by corporations, institutions, and other organizations.
For more information, please contact the publisher.

Cider Mill Press Book Publishers
"Where good books are ready for press"
PO Box 454
12 Spring Street
Kennebunkport, Maine 04046

Visit us online!
cidermillpress.com

Cover design by Cindy Butler
Interior design by Marit Snowball and Chris Russell
Typography: Apollo MT, Mrs. Eaves, Neutraface, Baskerville, Dakota
Image Credits: The Author: Jeremy D'Entremont; Douglas Ax, pg. 59; Jim Burrill, pg. 60; Steve Reed, pg. 61, 99-109; Rose Labrie, pg. 75; William O. Thomson, pg. 76, 88, 126; Herb Carpenter, pg. 81, 136; Barbara Finnemore, pg. 83; Debbie Jones, pg. 84; Bob Trapani, Jr. pg. 86, 87; Connie Small, pg. 94; Richard Winchester, pg. 111; Elinor DeWire, pg. 126; Friends of Flying Santa, pg. 128; Richard Beauchesne, pg. 144; Deb Cram, pg. 148, John Whalen, pg. 79, 110-111, 130. All other images used under official license from Shutterstock.com

Printed in China

1 2 3 4 5 6 7 8 9 0
First Edition

# Contents 〜〜〜〜〜〜〜〜〜〜〜〜

(photo by the author)

# Acknowledgments ～～～～～～～

It seems almost greedy for Portland Head Lighthouse to be blessed with such abundant beauty and history in a single package. The lighthouse tower is the third oldest standing lighthouse in the United States, and Portland Head is said to be the most visited and photographed lighthouse site in the world, with more than a million visitors each year. Edward Rowe Snow, the popular raconteur of the New England coast, aptly wrote in his book *Famous New England Lighthouses*, "Portland Head and its light seem to symbolize the state of Maine—rocky coast, breaking waves, sparkling water and clear, pure salt air."

The people who visit Portland Head each year would certainly agree with that summation, but the whole is bigger than the sum of its parts—the place is simply magic. I fell in love with Portland Head Light in the 1980s. One of my early visits was on August 7, 1989, when I attended the automation ceremony and a celebration of the bicentennial of America's lighthouse service. That event helped draw me toward lighthouse history as my life's work, and it deepened my love and appreciation for this very special place.

I need to thank many people for their contributions to this book, and because my association with Portland Head Light goes back so far, I'm afraid I'll miss some. For that I apologize.

A big thank-you to the Museum at Portland Head Light, and particularly the museum's director, Jeanne Gross. Jeanne and all the staff and volunteers of the museum have been wonderful to deal with over the years, and Jeanne made available many of the images seen in this book.

The Cape Elizabeth Historical Preservation Society was a major source of historical material and photographs, and I want to single out Jim Rowe and Jane

Beckwith for their kind assistance. Author/researcher J. Candace Clifford very generously shared vital research materials. Bob Trapani, Jr., executive director of the American Lighthouse Foundation, shared photos from his own collection and from the foundation's archives. Kathryn DiPhilippo, executive director of the South Portland Historical Society, provided some wonderful images from that organization's collection. Thanks also to the staffs of the Maine Lighthouse Museum, the National Archives, the Library of Congress, the U.S. Coast Guard Historian's Office, and the Maine Historic Preservation Commission.

Thanks also to Elinor DeWire, and to James W. Claflin of Kenrick Claflin & Son Nautical Antiques. And I want to express my gratitude to Tim Harrison and Kathleen Finnegan of *Lighthouse Digest*. Tim's book *Portland Head Light: A Pictorial Journey Through Time*, deserves special mention as a wonderful compilation of fact, lore, and images of this amazing location.

As always, the Cider Mill Press team has been a joy to work with. Many thanks to John Whalen, editor Mike Urban, designers Marit Snowball and Cindy Butler, and also Brittany Wason. And, as always, my wife, Charlotte Raczkowski, is deserving of more gratitude that I can ever express.

—**Jeremy D'Entremont**
Portsmouth, New Hampshire
April 2017

THE LIGHTHOUSE LIFTS
ITS MASSIVE MASONRY,
A PILLAR OF FIRE BY
NIGHT, OF CLOUD BY DAY.

—*Henry Wadsworth Longfellow,*
*"The Lighthouse"*

(photo by the author)

# Historical Background and the Call for a Lighthouse

The area of the southern Maine coast that is known today as the city of Portland was known as Machigonne, meaning "great neck," to the Algonquian Indians who once occupied the region. By around 1000 A.D., native people were coming to the area to gather fish and shellfish and to hunt for deer. The first European visitors, Portuguese and French traders, visited the area in the 1500s.

The native population was largely decimated by disease and warfare by the time the English explorer Christopher Levett established a settlement on Casco Bay in 1623. The bay's name is said to have originated with the Portuguese explorer Estêvão Gomes, who called it Bahía de Cascos on a 1525 map. "Casco" was a Portuguese word for a kind of helmet that Gomes felt had a similar shape to that of the bay.

In this 1779 map of Casco Bay, Portland Head is about halfway down, on the left side of the map.

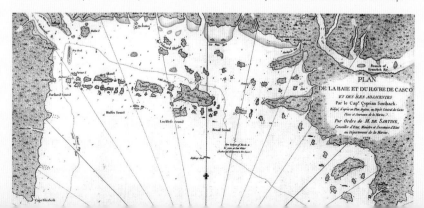

## CASCO BAY

Portland Head is near the southern border of Casco Bay, an inlet of the Gulf of Maine. The bay borders 13 coastal towns and cities, and the Casco Bay watershed covers a total area of 958 square miles. Depending on which source you believe, the name "Casco" comes either from the native Abenaki aucocisco, meaning "place of herons," or from a 1525 Portuguese map that dubbed the bay Bahía de Cascos, or "bay of helmets," after the helmet-shaped contours of the bay.

An English engineer proclaimed in 1700 that the bay had "as many islands as there are days in the year," leading to the nickname "Calendar Islands" and the mistaken belief that there are 365 islands in the bay. In reality, there are a little more than 200 islands, still an impressive number. The bay is also home to seven lighthouses in six locations: the Cape Elizabeth "Two Lights," Portland Head, Ram Island Ledge, Halfway Rock, Spring Point Ledge, and Portland Breakwater (Bug Light).

The bay's major islands are serviced by the ferries of Casco Bay Lines, based in Portland, and many residents commute to work in Portland via ferry. Peaks Island is the most populous island in the bay with more than 900 residents, swelling to more than 2,000 in summer. With restaurants, art galleries, and kayak rentals, Peaks Island is a major tourist draw in the warmer months.

Along with vibrant industry and shipping, Casco Bay supports approximately 850 species of marine life and 150 species of water birds.

Levett's settlement was short lived, but a more permanent English settlement was established by 1633. The fishing and trading village was called Casco, after the bay. Later, when the Massachusetts Bay Colony took control in 1658, the name of the area was changed to Falmouth, after Falmouth, England.

The bombardment of Falmouth by the Royal Navy in 1775 at the start of the American Revolution left the town in ruins, but a new era of prosperity began after the Revolution. A new town was founded on Falmouth Neck in 1786, named for the Isle of Portland in Dorsetshire, England.

Portland developed rapidly as an important shipping port and Maine's largest city. From 1820, when Maine became a state, until 1831, Portland served as the state capital. The name "Portland Head," given to a prominent headland almost three miles south of the entrance to Portland Harbor, was in use for more than a century before the city of Portland was named. Portland Head is part of Cape Elizabeth, now a town with a population of about 9,000.

Portland Head, often referred to as "Portland Point" in early accounts, was fortified during the American Revolution with cannons that were brought from Boston in July 1776. One officer and seven privates were put on guard. If they saw an enemy ship, they were told to "fire a gun on Portland Point as an alarm" and to use their "best endeavors to annoy" the approaching enemy.

There were no lighthouses on the coast of Maine when 74 merchants petitioned the Massachusetts government (Maine was part of Massachusetts at the time) in 1784 for a light at Portland Head to aid mariners approaching Portland Harbor.

At a Falmouth town meeting on May 25, 1785, Joseph Noyes was directed to look into the construction of a lighthouse at Portland Point for the "direction of vessels that may be on our coast, as soon as possible." Noyes

## WHERE CAPE ELIZABETH GOT ITS NAME

The name of Cape Elizabeth dates back to 1614–15, when the English explorer Captain John Smith visited and mapped the area. Back in England, the map was presented to Charles, Prince of Wales, with the suggestion that he should feel free to change any of the "barbarous names" Smith had provided. Charles named Cape Elizabeth for his sister, Princess Elizabeth (1596–1662). Cape Elizabeth separated from Falmouth and became a town in 1765.

Cape Ann, Massachusetts, the location of the towns of Gloucester and Rockport, was named by Prince Charles for his mother, Anne of Denmark.

Princess Elizabeth.

Cape Elizabeth, Me., Portland Head Light and Cliffs

4A H2170

(from the collection of the author)

had commanded a company based at Falmouth Neck during the Revolution, and he represented Falmouth in the General Court of Massachusetts from 1776 to 1786, with the exception of one year.

The deaths of two people—the captain and a young boy—in the February 1787 wreck of a Newbury-bound sloop at Bangs (now Cushing) Island near Portland Head led a local newspaper to blame the wreck on the lack of a lighthouse in the vicinity. "Does not this unhappy accident evince the necessity of having a lighthouse at the entrance to our harbor?" the writer asked.

The shipwreck and another petition led to the appropriation on June 26, 1789, of 150 pounds sterling (roughly $700) for a lighthouse by the General Court of Massachusetts. The resolution read:

*Whereas it will prove of great advantage to the commerce of this Commonwealth, as well as tend to the preservation of the lives of our fellow creatures, and more especially those carrying on the coasting trade in the eastern part of this State, that a light-house be established on Portland head, near Cape-Elizabeth, in the county of Cumberland.*

*Therefore Resolved, That the Commissary General, together with Joseph Noyes, Esq., Mr. John Fox, and Capt. Joseph McLellan, be and they are hereby invested with full power and authority to erect and build such light-house at Portland head, aforesaid, and of such heighth as the Committee shall think will be most beneficial, the same to be built of wood; provided the expence of erecting and building the same light-house shall not exceed the sum of one hundred and fifty pounds lawful money.*

*And it is further Resolved, That the expence of building the said light-house, shall be defrayed out of the monies which shall be received into the treasury of this Commonwealth, for the year one thousand seven hundred and eighty-eight.*

*And it is also further Resolved, That when the same light-house, shall be completed, the Commissary-General, shall provide suitable lights to be placed therein, and maintained in the same manner and out of the same funds, as other public lights of this Commonwealth are provided for and maintained.*

A newspaper ad on July 7, 1789, asked "any persons willing to furnish materials, or do the labour" to apply to the committee for erecting the lighthouse, which was headed by Joseph Noyes, John Fox, and Joseph McLellan.

A newspaper ad soliciting laborers to build a lighthouse at Portland Head.

Construction soon began, as reported in the *Essex Journal* of August 14, 1789:

*We are happy, says a correspondent, to inform the public that the erecting of a light house on Portland point is prosecuting with the utmost dispatch; so that we hope in a few weeks to see the edifice completed. The foundation is laid upon a rock, near the sea shore, and the basis, or bottom, is about twenty-five feet above the water at full tide.*

The appropriation was too small a sum to build anything substantial, and the project was soon stalled by insufficient funds, although members of the lighthouse committee added some of their own money in an attempt to complete the buildings. Governor John Hancock took an active interest; he requested money from the state treasurer for the building of "a small building for the keeper" on February 3, 1790, but the project remained stalled.

Meanwhile, Congress passed an act on August 7, 1789, that put the federal government in charge of lighthouses and other aids to navigation. Before that, lighthouse management had fallen to the individual colonies or states.

(photo by the author)

## THE 1789 LIGHTHOUSE ACT

From 1716 to 1789, the lighthouses in the American colonies were built and maintained by the individual colonies or states. The early lighthouses were largely paid for by dues that were based on the tonnage of vessels entering the ports. There were twelve lighthouses in service before 1789.

Virginia Representative James Madison raised the issue of federal support for lighthouses in April 1789. After debate and rewrites, an act was approved. On August 7, 1789, the first public works act of the first U.S. Congress, signed by President George Washington, provided:

*That all expenses which shall accrue from and after the 15th day of August 1789, in the necessary support, maintenance and repairs of all lighthouses, beacons, buoys and public piers erected, placed, or sunk before the passing of this Act, at the entrance of, or within any bay, inlet, harbor, or port of the United States, for rendering the navigation thereof easy and safe, shall be defrayed out of the treasury of the United*

*States; Provided nevertheless, That none of the said expenses shall continue to be so defrayed by the United States, after the expiration of one year of the day aforesaid, unless such lighthouses, beacons, buoys and public piers, shall in the mean time be ceded to and vested in the United States, by the state or states respectively in which the same may be, together with the jurisdiction of same.*

Portland Head Light has a unique distinction as the only American lighthouse that was built in part by a state government (Massachusetts) but was completed by the federal government in 1791. By 1797, all lighthouses had been transferred to the federal government.

In 1988, Senator John H. Chafee of Rhode Island sponsored a joint resolution designating August 7, 1989—the 200th anniversary of the Lighthouse Act—as "National Lighthouse Day." Congress has yet to designate a yearly observation of National Lighthouse Day, but many individual lighthouses hold special events each year on that date.

More than 30 members of the Portland Marine Society wrote to Congress in March 1790, in response to complaints, such as this, from ship captains: "Our Navigation is exposed to great danger from the Light House upon Portland Head not having a Lanthorn [lantern] large enough for the purpose and not being properly attended. And also from a number of dangerous Ledges near the entrance of the Harbour, which are not provided with Buoys."

Alexander Hamilton, the secretary of the Treasury Department and thus in charge of the nation's lighthouses, wrote to General Benjamin Lincoln, the local customs collector and lighthouse superintendent, on June 24, 1790, with the following request: "If you could procure . . . an Account of the Cost of the Light House, so far as it is built—the height to which it is carried—the height to which it is proposed to be carried, and an estimate of the expence that will attend the Completion of it, I shall be obliged to you."

Lincoln wrote back on July 3: "I have seen one of the Gentlemen to whom was committed the building the light-house at Portland and find that the house is fifty-eight feet in height that it must be raised Eight feet higher which will cost about one hundred dollars. The whole expence which has been incurred for the land the Light-house and for a dwelling-house for the keeper amounts to thirteen hundred dollars . . . The expence to finish the whole will, from the best light I can obtain, amount to about seven hundred dollars . . . "

Soon after, the lighthouse was ceded to the federal government, and Congress authorized its completion—provided it cost no more than $1,500—on August 10, 1790.

The act authorizing the building of the lighthouse, signed by Secretary of State Thomas Jefferson.

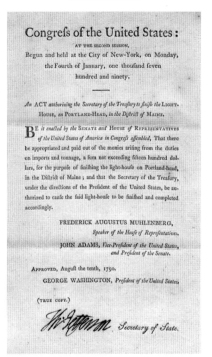

Hamilton wrote to General Lincoln on October 4, 1790, telling him that it was hoped the work could be completed before winter. President George Washington then wrote to Hamilton on October 12 to let him know that the project was "perfectly agreeable"

to him. Washington remarked that it should be possible to build the tower from rubblestone found in the fields and shores of Cape Elizabeth, and that the stone could be "handled nicely when hauled by oxen on a drag."

Two local masons, Jonathan Bryant and John Nichols, were hired to complete the rubblestone lighthouse under the direction of General Benjamin Lincoln, the local customs collector and lighthouse superintendent. Bryant owned a lime kiln operation at the foot of India Street in Portland.

When it was realized that the light would be blocked from the south by a headland, Lincoln decided that the tower should be 72 feet high to the base of the lantern, which was several feet higher than the original plans. Bryant resigned over the change, and Nichols finished the lighthouse and a small dwelling in late 1790. By November 10, the tower was completed except for the installation of a lantern.

On November 27, 1790, the newspaper Osborne's *New Hampshire Spy* reported that the stonework was "extremely well executed," doing honor to "Mr. Nichols, the master builder." It was reported that the lantern was being prepared and would "probably be raised and lighted by the first of next month."

In early December 1790, Captain Joseph McClellan wrote in a letter that "neither heat or cold" had "abated at any one time the goal of the workmen" and added that it was the desire of everyone to have the work swiftly completed.

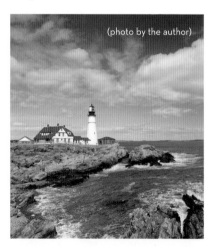

(photo by the author)

(photo by the author)

# Early Days, 1791–1869

At the end of October 1790, a petition was submitted by Portland mariners and businessmen supporting the appointment of a "very suitable person," Captain Joseph Greenleaf, a 51-year-old native of Portland and a veteran of the American Revolution, to be keeper of the new lighthouse. President Washington subsequently approved the appointment on January 7, 1791: "Know ye, that I have appointed Joseph Greenleaf, Keeper of the Lighthouse at Portland in the District of Maine in the State of Massachusetts, to exercise, and fulfill the Power, and Duties of Office; and to hold with the same authorities, privilege, and emoluments thereunto . . . "

Secretary Hamilton wrote to Benjamin Lincoln, telling him to be sure to "make provision for the requisite supplies of oil, wicks, etc." for the new keeper. Construction was completed and the light went into service on January 10, 1791, with whale oil lamps showing a fixed white light from a copper lantern atop the 72-foot tower.

## WHAT ARE OUR OLDEST LIGHTHOUSES?

Portland Head Light, completed in 1791, is the third oldest standing lighthouse tower in the United States, after the extant towers at Sandy Hook, New Jersey (1764) and Boston Harbor (1783). (The original Boston Light, built in 1716, was destroyed by the British in 1776.)

Portland Head Light was partially built by the Commonwealth of Massachusetts, but it was the first lighthouse to begin service under the management of the federal government. The lighthouse at Cape Henry, Virginia, was the first lighthouse to be built entirely by the federal government; it also went into service in 1791.

The following notice appeared in newspapers:

*Last Monday evening, the Light-House on Portland Head, at the entrance of this harbour, was lighted. The building is built with stone and lime—is seventy-two feet high, exclusive of the lanthorn. The following DIRECTIONS are given for coming into this harbour.*

*Bring the light to bear N.N.W. then run for it, allowing it a small distance on the larboard hand; and when abreast of the same, then run N. by W. This course will give good anchorage from half a mile to one and an half.*

*A particular survey will soon be taken, the public will then have notice of the bearings of the light from the different Rocks and Shoals, together with directions how far vessels may stand, either East or West, when beating in.*

A close look at the lighthouse tower clearly shows the original rubblestone construction. (Photo by the author.)

Greenleaf died of an apparent stroke while in his boat in Portland Harbor on October 3, 1795. Before the end of October, President Washington approved the appointment of Reuben Freeman as the new keeper. A recommendation signed by local merchants had called Freeman an "active" and "faithful man," who was "very suitable to fill the place" that Greenleaf's death had left open.

There were multiple men with the name Reuben Freeman in the area at the time, but it appears that the Reuben Freeman who served a few months as keeper was from the same prominent local family as a later keeper, Joshua Freeman.

According to some sources, David Duncan served as keeper for a few months, but this seems unlikely; Duncan was the keeper down the coast at Portsmouth Harbor Lighthouse in New Hampshire from 1793 to 1820. In any case, Barzillai Delano was appointed keeper at Portland Head in early March 1796.

(photo by the author)

Correspondence from Tench Coxe, commissioner of the revenue, in June and July 1797 indicated that too much sand may have been used in the tower's mortar, which could be "picked out" and had "fallen much," that the lantern was "much too small," and that dampness in the tower produced vapor that clouded the lantern glass and dimmed the light.

The lantern was so small that the keeper didn't have room to move around the lamps to clean the glass, and the lantern gallery (the outside deck around the lantern) was too small to allow him to clean the outside of the glass. Coxe directed that the stonework be repointed, inside and out, "with the best mortar," after the old mortar had been "picked with an instrument."

Barzillai Delano wrote to the local superintendent in 1809, complaining of leaks in the tower caused by the action of the seas against the tower, which had washed out much of the mortar. Delano also complained that it was difficult walking between the keeper's house and the tower, because the space between them was steep and rocky and often frozen over. Wooden sheathing was suggested as a remedy for the leaks, but the plan was never carried out.

By 1810, the woodwork in the lighthouse and keeper's house was damp and rotting. Part of the problem was that the keeper was storing a year's supply of oil in one room, which put great stress on the floor. Repairs were made to the house, an oil shed was built, and a cistern was installed around the same time.

The lighthouse remained active through the War of 1812, and Delano kept an eye out for the approach of British vessels. "Night after night," according to a newspaper article, "during those troublous times the light guided into port the Yankee privateersmen."

The tower continued to have problems with leaks. In November 1812, Winslow Lewis—a contractor from Massachusetts who built many early lighthouses—offered the opinion that the upper 22 feet of the tower had been poorly constructed. The copper lantern, which was only five feet in diameter, was also badly constructed.

# WINSLOW LEWIS

Winslow Lewis is sometimes portrayed as a villain in the history of American lighthouses. He was, in fact, a shrewd businessman—more opportunist than scoundrel.

Lewis, who was born in Wellfleet on Cape Cod in 1770, was a sea captain who developed a new system of lighting for lighthouses. He used a variant of the Argand lamp—an efficient oil lamp that was popular in Europe—and paired the lamps with parabolic reflectors and magnifying lenses. Lewis gained a patent for his system in 1810, and the "Lewis Lamp" was chosen as a standard in American lighthouses. Based out of an office on State Street in Boston, Lewis made a great deal of money off his innovation despite many problems with the system. The copper reflectors warped and the silver coating rubbed off, the lamps were prone to "sooting up," and the lenses made the light worse instead of better.

Lewis earned the trust of Stephen Pleasonton, the treasury official in charge of the U.S. Lighthouse Establishment from 1820 to 1852. As a result, his lighting system remained in exclusive use until the formation of the new U.S. Lighthouse Board in 1852 led to the adoption of the much more efficient Fresnel lens. Ironically, it was the seminal report of the civil engineer I. W. P. Lewis, Winslow's nephew, that paved the way for many improvements in America's lighthouse administration and technology.

During his long career, Lewis also built many lighthouses and associated buildings. He won the contracts because he was the low bidder, but his construction methods were largely substandard. Only a handful of his lighthouses remain standing, including Sapelo Island Lighthouse in Georgia. Winslow Lewis died in 1850.

Winslow Lewis. (Courtesy of the U.S. Lighthouse Society)

Lewis recommended the reduction of the tower's height by 20 feet, followed by the construction of a new lantern. "The building then would be substantial, and they would have a light equal to the importance of the situation of it," he wrote. Lewis carried out these changes himself in 1813,

(photo by the author)

along with the installation of a system of lamps and reflectors that he had designed, at a cost of $2,100. About 25 feet of stonework at the top of the tower was removed. Apparently, the fact that a headland blocked the light to the south was no longer of great concern.

The contractor Henry Dyer of Cape Elizabeth built a new keeper's house in 1816 for $1,175. The one-story stone cottage was 20 feet by 34 feet and had two rooms, an attached kitchen, and an attic. The kitchen ell was attached to outbuildings, which in turn were joined to the tower. The joining of the house to the tower answered Delano's complaints, making passage between the two buildings much easier.

Barzillai Delano died in June 1820, three months after Maine had been admitted as a state. The superintendence of local lighthouses was transferred at that time to Isaac Ilsley, the collector of customs at Portland.

Joshua Freeman, who would become known for his jovial hospitality, followed Delano as keeper. A year later in 1821, the light was made brighter by an increase from 10 to 15 lamps, a project that was again carried out by Winslow Lewis. The new lighting system consisted of 15 oil lamps paired with parabolic reflectors; the reflectors varied in diameter from 14 $\frac{3}{4}$ inches to 16 $\frac{3}{4}$ inches.

Freeman died on January 2, 1840, at the age of 76. Richard Lee succeeded Freeman as keeper at a yearly salary of $350. Lee was in charge when the civil engineer I. W. P. Lewis (Winslow Lewis's nephew) visited in August 1842 for an important report to Congress on the state of the nation's lighthouses. Lewis found the tower and keeper's house in bad condition:

*Tower of rubble masonry, forty-three feet nine inches high, laid up in lime mortar of an inferior quality, base resting on the uneven surface of a ledge; masonry in a bad condition; pointing cracked off, and joints open; mortar soft and sandy; interior wood work rotten—staircase and floor beams very much so; wooden roof coppered, leaks around the eaves.*

# THE U.S. LIGHTHOUSE BOARD

In 1852, management of the lighthouses of the United States passed to the new U.S. Lighthouse Board, ending decades of complaints of mismanagement under the Lighthouse Establishment of the Treasury Department.

On March 3, 1851, Congress passed an act that stated:

*The Secretary of the Treasury is authorized and required to cause a board to be convened at as early a day as may be practical after the passage of that act to be comprised of two officers of the Navy of high rank, two officers of Engineers of the Army, and such civil officers of scientific attainments as may be under the orders or at the disposition of the Treasury Department, and a junior officer of the Navy to act as Secretary to said board, whose duty it shall be under instructions from the Treasury Department to inquire into the condition of the*

*Lighthouse Establishment of the United States, and make a general detailed report and programme to guide legislation in extending and improving our present system of construction, illumination, inspection, and superintendence.*

Under the U.S. Lighthouse Board, technological advances took place almost immediately, including the adoption of the efficient Fresnel lens in American lighthouses. Many advances in fog signal technology also took place in the 1850s.

In 1910, the Lighthouse Board gave way to a new Bureau of Lighthouses, or Lighthouse Service, under the Department of Commerce. Appointed by President Taft, George Putnam became the commissioner of lighthouses for 25 years. In 1939, the Bureau of Lighthouses was merged with the United States Coast Guard.

*Dwelling-house of rubble masonry, laid up in lime mortar of bad quality; roof shingled. Walls of house cracked in several places, and very leaky; two rooms on first floor, and two chambers in attic; no sink in the kitchen, and oven broken down . . . whole establishment requires repairing.*

Lewis reported that the 15 lamps and corresponding reflectors in the octagonal lantern—installed by his uncle in 1813—were out of alignment. Four of the lamps faced the land "to no

purpose," and the whole arrangement was "defective." Lewis recommended fewer lamps more properly aligned. He considered Portland Head a "very important establishment," but the station's condition was "far inferior to what such a locality requires."

A separate inspection by the local lighthouse superintendent in 1843 called the lighting apparatus "clean and in good order," although it did mention some of the same problems with the condition of the lighthouse tower and keeper's house.

A new system of 13 lamps, each backed by a 21-inch reflector was installed along with a new lantern and a new lantern deck in 1850. In August of that year, an inspection report from the local superintendent indicated that many of the problems noted by I. W. P. Lewis still persisted: "This lighthouse is built of stone of all description— round, flat, &c. The mortar has become dead; consequently the rain drives through. . . . Dwelling-house is built of stone and is very leaky; it wants pointing, whitewashing, and painting."

An examination by the newly commissioned U.S. Lighthouse Board in 1851 revealed that the new reflectors were already badly scratched. John F. Watts, who had been keeper for two years, had been poorly trained. The oil was of poor quality, the house was leaky and cracking, and rats were undermining the tower. There was some sort of foghorn at the station, according to the report, that was sounded by "private arrangement" by the keeper for passing steamers.

This was, perhaps, a low point for Portland Head Lighthouse, but things would soon get better. The establishment of the new, more efficient U.S. Lighthouse Board in 1852 led to many improvements in the years that followed. A fourth-order Fresnel lens replaced the old multiple lamps and reflectors in 1855. In the same year, the tower was lined with brick, and a cast-iron spiral stairway was added. Also, on July 27, 1855, the following Notice to Mariners was issued: "Notice is hereby given that a Fog Bell weighing 1,500 pounds, to be rung by machinery, has been erected at Portland Head Lighthouse. It will be rung in foggy weather hereafter and will strike every half-minute. It is placed on a wooden frame 24 feet high and is about 60 feet above the level of the sea."

(photo by the author)

This photo from 1858 is the earliest known photo of Portland Head Light. The 1816 dwelling can be seen, as well as the 1855 fog bell tower. The lighthouse tower is just behind the dwelling.
(Courtesy of the Maine Historic Preservation Commission)

Circa 1859 photo of Portland Head Light
(National Archives)

Portland Harbor was the scene of some activity during the Civil War, most notably a battle in June 1863. A Confederate raider, the *Tacony*, was being pursued by the Union navy. The Confederates on the *Tacony* captured the *Archer*, a Maine fishing schooner, and burned the *Tacony*. They sailed the *Archer* past Portland Head Light into Portland Harbor, where they seized a revenue cutter, the *Caleb Cushing*. After a naval battle with the steamer *Forest City*, the Confederates were captured. They were imprisoned for a time at Fort Preble in South Portland.

(photo by the author)

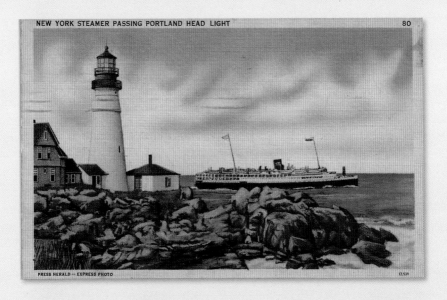

PRESS HERALD — EXPRESS PHOTO

12,519

COPR. DETROIT PHOTOGRAPHIC CO.

6679 PORTLAND HEAD LIGHT, PORTLAND, ME.

Portland, Me.--Portland Head Light.

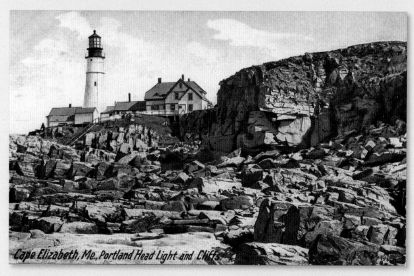

Cape Elizabeth, Me., Portland Head Light and Cliffs

# WRECK OF THE BOHEMIAN

The steamer *Bohemian*, a three-masted iron vessel, departed Liverpool, England, on February 4, 1864, bound for Portland with 219 passengers—200 predominantly Irish immigrants in steerage and 19 cabin-class passengers—and a crew of 99 men.

On February 23, it appeared that the tedious voyage was coming to an end, as the *Bohemian* made her way along Cape Elizabeth toward Portland Harbor. It was a hazy evening. A little after 7:00 p.m., a lookout informed the captain that he could see two lights on shore—one fixed and one flashing. Borland knew that the lights were the Cape Elizabeth Light Station, known locally as Two Lights. The unusual atmospheric conditions, however, tricked Borland into believing he was much farther offshore than was actually the case.

At about 8:00 p.m., there was a light shudder, and then a more pronounced one. The 295-foot ship had struck Alden's Rock, a menacing obstruction in shallow water about two miles southeast of Cape Elizabeth's Two Lights. The jagged ledge ripped a hole in the engine room. Within about 10 minutes, the rising waters stopped the engines.

Borland ordered the *Bohemian*'s six lifeboats readied as the steamer began to sink. As the No. 2 boat was being lowered, a pin broke. One end of the boat fell precipitously, violently heaving many passengers into the freezing ocean waves. Accounts vary, but it appears that 16 people died in the accident with the No. 2 lifeboat.

All the other lifeboats and their occupants made it safely to shore. As the last boats were launched, some passengers jumped into the water and attempted to climb into them. One who jumped was a woman who had lashed her infant to her shoulders. The woman and baby were rescued, but many others who jumped drowned. Some of the lifeboats returned before midnight and the rest of the passengers were safely removed.

All told, 42 people, including two crewmembers, perished. The Portland Board of Trade undertook a thorough examination of the area's rocks and shoals to make sure suitable buoys marked them. The wreck of the *Bohemian* was also a contributing factor to improvements made at Portland Head Lighthouse. The tower was subsequently raised 20 feet, and a more powerful lens was installed.

The *Bohemian* tragedy is recalled in a poignant mural, *Shipwreck at Night*, painted by Alzira Peirce, on public display at the post office in South Portland.

This mural of the wreck of the *Bohemian* by artist Alzira Peirce is on display at the South Portland Post Office.

Nineteenth-century engraving of the wreck of the *Bohemian* (Collection of the author)

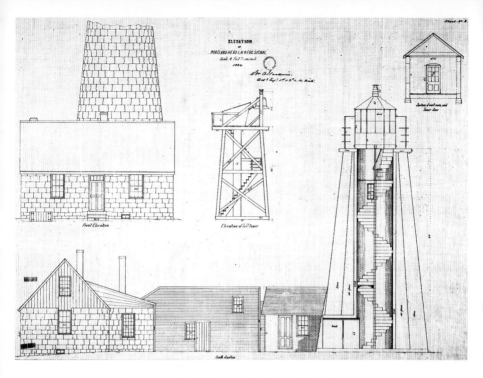

1864 drawings of the lighthouse and bell tower (National Archives)

Following the 1864 wreck of the Liverpool vessel *Bohemian*, in which 40 immigrants died, Portland Head Light was further improved. The tower was raised 20 feet with an addition constructed of brick, and a more powerful second-order Fresnel lens was installed. The new lens began service on December 1, 1864, and it was reported that the light was visible "from the deck of a vessel 15 feet above the water, at a distance of 17 miles."

The 1865 annual report of the Lighthouse Board stated, "It is believed now that the entrance to this harbor is so completely lighted that navigation in and out is attended with little or no danger."

# HENRY WADSWORTH LONGFELLOW AND "THE LIGHTHOUSE"

Henry Wadsworth Longfellow, beloved American poet, was born in Portland, Maine, in 1807. Longfellow's grandfather had been one of the founders of Bowdoin College in Brunswick, Maine, and Henry entered Bowdoin as a student at the age of 15. He eventually became a professor there and later at Harvard College. He lived much of the time in Cambridge, Massachusetts, after 1836.

In 1847, he visited the Two Lights in Cape Elizabeth and climbed one of the towers. It's generally believed that he had visited Portland Head Light, which was about five miles from his childhood home, by the 1840s and that it served as an inspiration for his 1849 poem "The Lighthouse." Although not as famous as his bestselling works that included "The Song of Hiawatha" and "Paul Revere's Ride," "The Lighthouse" is an enduring, much-loved poem.

Later in life, Longfellow visited Portland often, and it was not unusual for him to walk to Portland Head Lighthouse. Robert Thayer Sterling, who was a keeper in later years at Portland Head as well as an author, wrote that the poet would bow as a salute to Keeper Joshua Freeman Strout, and would then "scan the ocean and its shores." John Strout, a descendant of the Strout family of keepers, has written, "Longfellow would sit with Joshua, and both would chat and sip cool drinks prepared by my great grandmother."

A rock that was said to be his favorite place to sit and soak in the salty ambience is now marked with a sign that bears part of his poem "The Lighthouse."

Henry Wadsworth Longfellow, photographed by Julia Margaret Cameron in 1868.
(Wikimedia Commons)

## The Lighthouse

*The rocky ledge runs far into the sea,*
*And on its outer point, some miles away,*
*The Lighthouse lifts its massive masonry,*
*A pillar of fire by night, of cloud by day.*

*Even at this distance I can see the tides,*
*Upheaving, break unheard along its base,*
*A speechless wrath, that rises and subsides*
*In the white lip and tremor of the face.*

*And as the evening darkens, lo! how bright,*
*Through the deep purple of the twilight air,*
*Beams forth the sudden radiance of its light*
*With strange, unearthly splendor in the glare!*

*Not one alone; from each projecting cape*
*And perilous reef along the ocean's verge,*
*Starts into life a dim, gigantic shape,*
*Holding its lantern o'er the restless surge.*

Like the great giant Christopher it stands
  Upon the brink of the tempestuous wave,
Wading far out among the rocks and sands,
  The night-o'ertaken mariner to save.

And the great ships sail outward and return,
  Bending and bowing o'er the billowy swells,
And ever joyful, as they see it burn,
  They wave their silent welcomes and farewells.

They come forth from the darkness, and their sails
  Gleam for a moment only in the blaze,
And eager faces, as the light unveils,
  Gaze at the tower, and vanish while they gaze.

The mariner remembers when a child,
  On his first voyage, he saw it fade and sink;
And when, returning from adventures wild,
  He saw it rise again o'er ocean's brink.

Steadfast, serene, immovable, the same
  Year after year, through all the silent night
Burns on forevermore that quenchless flame,
  Shines on that inextinguishable light!

It sees the ocean to its bosom clasp
  The rocks and sea-sand with the kiss of peace;
It sees the wild winds lift it in their grasp,
  And hold it up, and shake it like a fleece.

The startled waves leap over it; the storm
  Smites it with all the scourges of the rain,
And steadily against its solid form
  Press the great shoulders of the hurricane.

The sea-bird wheeling round it, with the din
  Of wings and winds and solitary cries,
Blinded and maddened by the light within,
  Dashes himself against the glare, and dies.

A new Prometheus, chained upon the rock,
  Still grasping in his hand the fire of Jove,
It does not hear the cry, nor heed the shock,
  But hails the mariner with words of love.

"Sail on!" it says, "sail on, ye stately ships!
  And with your floating bridge the ocean span;
Be mine to guard this light from all eclipse,
  Be yours to bring man nearer unto man!"

This rock, said to be a favorite resting spot for
the poet Henry Wadsworth Longfellow, is marked
with a plaque that includes part of his poem *The
Lighthouse*. (Photo by the author)

# The Strout Era, 1869–1928

Joshua Freeman Strout, named for the earlier keeper Joshua Freeman, became keeper in 1869 at a salary of $620 per year. It was the start of a family dynasty at Portland Head that would span nearly six decades.

Keeper Joshua Freeman Strout (courtesy of the Museum at Portland Head Light)

Although Portland Head was a plum among assignments for lighthouse keepers, life wasn't always tranquil. A hurricane on September 8, 1869, knocked the fog bell from its perch into the ocean, nearly taking Joshua Strout with it. During the same storm, the Gloucester fishing schooner *Helen Eliza* was wrecked at Peaks Island in Casco Bay, with the loss of 11 crewmen.

An enclosed pyramidal tower replaced the old skeletal bell tower in the following year. A 2,000-pound bell from Sheffield, England, was installed with a Stevens striking mechanism.

The bell didn't remain in use much longer; it was replaced in late 1871 by a fog trumpet formerly used on Monhegan Island. The bell remained in place as an auxiliary signal. A

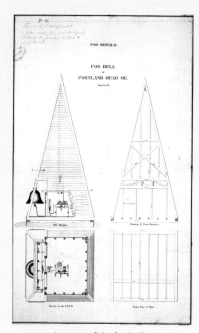

1872 drawings of the fog bell tower
(National Archives)

A 1901 fog bell is on display outside the
keeper's house. (photo by the author)

Circa 1870 photo, with the 1869 fog bell tower
(courtesy of the Cape Elizabeth Historical
Preservation Society)

Notice to Mariners in December 1871 announced that the new signal would "give a blast of eight seconds duration, with intervals between the blasts of 40 seconds, during thick weather."

Portland Head was always a tourist attraction, and a favorite pastime of visitors was watching the crashing surf during storms. A tremendous storm swept the Maine coast in November 1871, doing great damage to Portland's wharves. The *Eastern Argus* reported that many people went to Portland Head to view the spectacular surf, and Keeper Joshua Strout "kindly furnished every reasonable facility for the accommodation of the sight seekers." The sound of the "mountainous billows" striking the rocky shore was described as "a roar like the voice of many Niagara's."

# FORT WILLIAMS

Portland Head Lighthouse's most conspicuous neighbor is sprawling Fort Williams, which was an important military installation beginning in 1872. The fort was named in 1899 for Brevet Major General Seth Williams, assistant adjutant general of the Union's Army of the Potomac during the Civil War.

Fort Williams was greatly expanded from the 1880s into the early 1900s, with three gun batteries and many support buildings, including barracks, officers' quarters, hospital, gymnasium, commissary, bakery, chapel, fire station, and more. Anti-aircraft guns were added during World War I, and the fort was fully manned by the Coast Artillery Corps and the Maine National Guard.

During World War II, the fort became the headquarters for the defense of Portland Harbor. In 1950, Fort Williams became the logistical and administrative support installation for all military units in Maine. A short time later, the fort became a training site for the Air National Guard.

After the fort closed in 1962, the property was sold to the town of Cape Elizabeth. Most of the fort buildings were demolished, but a few remain. As you drive into the park, the large concrete structure ahead of you on the left overlooking the water is Battery Keyes, built in 1906. The battery had two three-inch rapid-fire guns on pedestal mounts, capable of firing 15-pound shells as far as four and one-half miles. Between the lighthouse and the primary parking lot is Battery Blair (1903), which was mounted with two 12-inch guns on disappearing carriages, designed to defend against battleships and cruisers.

The grounds were dedicated as Fort Williams Park in 1979. The 90-acre park, free to the public, boasts tennis courts, a basketball court, baseball field, physical fitness course, picnic facilities, and plenty of room for walking, running, and dog walking. The Beach to Beacon 10k, an annual road race that attracts several thousand runners, begins at Crescent Beach State Park and ends at Fort Williams Park.

In his 1876 book, *Portland and Vicinity*, Edward H. Elwell reported that a few years earlier a party had gone to Portland Head to watch the waves during a gale—possibly the storm of November 1871. Two carriage drivers who had taken the group out ventured too far onto the rocks and were swept away. Their bodies were recovered several days later.

Another great storm swept the Portland area in early December 1878. The *Portland Daily Press* reported that glass in the lighthouse lantern was broken by the storm, and Joshua Strout said he hadn't seen the sea so violent in 14 years.

A report in May 1882 by Colonel C. E. Blunt, engineer for the U.S. Lighthouse Board, indicated that

Portland Head Light had lost its value as a major seacoast light, as it served local maritime interests exclusively, particularly after the completion of Halfway Rock Light far offshore in Casco Bay in 1871. Also, Portland Head's 1864 brick addition was reported to be dilapidated, and the lantern was in poor condition.

For those reasons, it was decided in early 1883 that the tower would be shortened. Captain Charles Deering of the steamer *Lewiston* wrote to the Lighthouse Board in April 1883, protesting the change in the belief that the light had been "very serviceable" as it was, but the decision was final. The tower was shortened by 20 feet in May 1883, and a new lantern and a fourth-order lens were installed.

At the same time, the fuel for the light was changed from lard oil to kerosene. Major Charles W. Raymond, an engineer for the U.S. Lighthouse Board, examined the light on June 1, 1883, and said he was satisfied that the light was sufficiently powerful.

There were many complaints about the lowered, weaker light. Petitions

Circa 1883, during the brief period before the tower was again raised in height
(courtesy of the Cape Elizabeth Historical and Preservation Society)

Surf and Cliffs near Portland Head

(from the collection of the author)

An 1884 photo showing scaffolding around the tower while it was being raised in height (courtesy of the Maine Historic Preservation Commission)

"praying for the restoration" of the lighthouse with the names of 725 shipmasters, ship owners, and pilots were sent to Congress in March 1884, but to no avail. Vice Admiral S. C. Rowan, chairman of the Lighthouse Board, stated on April 1, 1884, that he and the other members of the board saw no reason "why this light should be restored to its former condition as regards the order of the light and the height of the tower."

When a fishing schooner, the *C & B Morse*, was wrecked off Cape Elizabeth, it was reported that the captain had mistaken a light on the shore for the truncated light in the lighthouse. A newspaper reporter blamed the accident squarely on the "folly" of the decision to lower the lighthouse.

Less than two years after it was shortened, the tower was again raised 20 feet, and a second-order lens was again installed. The improved fixed-white light went into service on January 15, 1885. The brick addition installed at that time remains in place today.

One of the most infamous of Maine shipwrecks occurred on Christmas Eve, 1886—that of the brig *Annie C. Maguire*. No loss of life resulted from the disaster, but the wreck is largely remembered because it happened on the rocks right next to the lighthouse, providing a memorable photo opportunity for countless visitors for several days before the ship finally broke apart and sank.

In August 1887, a caloric (hot-air) engine for the fog signal was moved from Boston Light to Portland Head to replace an engine that had worn out. In 1888, a new brick fog signal building, slightly more than 20 feet-by-20 feet in size, was erected to replace the one that had been badly damaged by the great wave of December 1887. The fog signal's characteristic was changed in 1896 to a two-second blast every 15 seconds. Three years later, it was changed again to five-second blasts separated by 15-second intervals.

The Strouts performed a dramatic rescue during a storm on November 30, 1887, when the schooner *D. W. Hammond* was driven onto the rocks

north of the station. The vessel had left Portsmouth, New Hampshire, for Rockland, Maine, and was carrying a cargo of flour, clay, sugar, and other goods. As the winds were increasing, the captain decided to pull into the shelter of Portland Harbor, but he ran into a dangerous area known as Trundy's Reef. According to a newspaper account, the sails were torn to shreds, and the captain was "knocked insensible" by a swinging boom.

Joseph Strout and his brother Gilman ("Gil"), who was also an assistant keeper, got a line to the nearly frozen captain and two crewmen from

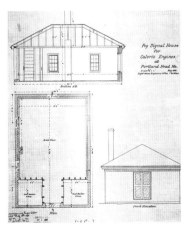

1888 plans for the new fog signal building (National Archives)

Circa 1880s, after the tower was raised in height to its present configuration (courtesy of the Cape Elizabeth Historical and Preservation Society)

(photo by the author)

# WRECK OF THE *ANNIE C. MAGUIRE*

The wreck of the *Annie C. Maguire*. (courtesy of the Museum at Portland Head Light)

The ship we know as the *Annie C. Maguire* led two lives. The first incarnation was the extreme clipper ship *Golden State*, built on the East River in New York City in 1852–53. In early 1883, after an unusually long 30-year career in the China trade, the *Golden State* was converted to bark rigging.

Renamed the *Annie C. Maguire*, the bark sailed under the British flag in North and South America during the 1883-86 period. The *Maguire* was headed home to Quebec in December 1886, after leaving Buenos Aires, Argentina. On board with Captain Daniel O'Niel were his wife and 12-year-old son, two mates, and 13 crewmen.

The *Maguire* entered Casco Bay at about 11:00 p.m. on Christmas Eve, with the intention of riding out the bad weather in Portland Harbor. A heavy sea was visible outside Portland Harbor that day, as a winter storm was raging offshore. At Portland Head Light, a few miles from the harbor's entrance, Keeper Joshua Freeman Strout was asked by a sheriff's officer to keep an eye out for the ship, in case the captain decided to duck into Portland Harbor to take shelter from the storm.

Newspaper reports in the following days said that "rain was falling in torrents." Joshua's son, Joseph Strout, assistant keeper at the time, claimed it was windy but not raining. "The wind was howling a gale," he said. "It was Christmas Eve, you know, and I guess even Santa Claus was afraid to be out."

Strangely, in another interview in 1929, Joseph Strout said it was snowing so hard "you couldn't see a hand in front of you," but that the night was calm and there was no wind. He said his father was on watch in the lighthouse and the "world as silent as death." Windy or not, in both interviews Strout stressed the fact that it was snowing heavily.

At about 11:30 p.m., as Joshua Strout kept watch in the lighthouse tower, Joseph was preparing for bed. Joshua later recalled that he heard the shouts of crewmen aboard the *Maguire* as they tried to veer away from the rocks. Captain O'Niel later said that he could see the light from the lighthouse, but his helmsman misjudged the distance to the light because of the storm.

Suddenly, Joshua burst through the door of the keeper's house and exclaimed to his son, "All hands turn out! There's a ship ashore in the dooryard!" Joseph fumbled as he put his socks and shoes back on, and then bolted down the stairs a half-dozen at a time.

When he emerged from the house, Joseph Strout was amazed to see the ship on the ledges no more than 100 feet from the lighthouse tower, listing to one side. As soon as it had run onto the ledge, the captain had the crew take down the sails and lower the anchors. According to some accounts, Mary Strout shed light on the scene by burning blankets that had 1 been cut into strips and soaked in kerosene.

There are varying versions of how the Strouts rescued the people from the ship. In 1927, Joseph Strout said that the water was calm enough to permit the men "to jump ashore, almost without help, so hard on the ledge was the vessel." Some, including Robert T. Sterling in his book *Lighthouses of the Maine Coast*, have claimed the Strouts rescued everyone with a breeches buoy. A newspaper account in the *Boston Globe* stated that the Strouts put a ladder across to the ship, and that all aboard made it safely across the ladder to solid ground.

Mary Strout soon had hot coffee and food ready for the shipwreck victims in an engine room. They were ravenous after their long voyage with little more to eat than salt beef and macaroni. Joseph Strout said in 1929:

*The day before we had killed eight chickens so that we could have a big feed on Christmas. Ma made all eight into the best pie you ever tasted. But it didn't make no impression on that crew of three-quarter starved blotters though. I only got one plateful. But we should worry. A feller doesn't get wrecked often, and when it happens where he can eat after starving for weeks, you can't blame him for passing his plate until it's all gone. Once they got that chicken pie into them, the whole gang wanted to stay. They loafed around three days and ate most of the food we had while Dad did his best to convince them that we were a lighthouse and not a life saving station.*

Joshua Strout was put in charge of the ship by the deputy sheriff, and the wreck was soon surveyed. The *New York Times* reported on December 27 that the *Maguire*'s bottom was "badly stove." It was thought that the ship would likely break apart in the next storm, so Joshua Strout ordered that everything removable be brought ashore as quickly as possible. The *Maguire* broke apart in a storm about a week after the wreck.

Joseph Strout's son, John A. Strout, was born at the lighthouse in 1891. He followed the family tradition by becoming an assistant keeper under his father, on his 21st birthday. On the same day, John A. Strout painted an inscription on the ledge where the *Maguire* was wrecked. He first had to chip much of the huge rock to make a flat surface on which to paint, and the lettering was applied with a mixture of paint, mortar, and sand.

The exact wording and spelling of the inscription have varied over the years and a wooden cross that once topped the rock is gone, but the tradition of repainting it continues as a reminder of the Christmas Eve when a once proud ship almost hit the lighthouse.

(photo by the author)

Circa 1880s (courtesy of the Cape Elizabeth Historical and Preservation Society)

the vessel. They reached shore and were rushed inside the keeper's house, where they were revived through the efforts of Mary Strout and her daughter-in-law.

Just a month later, on December 28, 1887, Portland was pelted by a storm that brought heavy rain and winds of 50 miles per hour. The gale was nothing extraordinary until about 9:30 p.m., when the Strouts watched in horror as they saw a "great wave" in the shape of a pyramid approaching the light station through the rain. A farmer about two miles away was quoted in newspapers: "When the wave was coming it made a fearful roar, but when it struck the cliffs, it seemed as though it fairly smashed them to pieces . . . . Another such gigantic blow would have done woeful damage along the shore."

The wave struck the outer line of rocks, cleared the top of the lighthouse, and smashed into the fog signal building. "Great iron stays were snapped as though they had been pipe stems," according to a newspaper account. When the wave receded, it took everything that wasn't secured back to the sea with it, including boulders weighing tons.

The old stone dwelling was removed in 1891 to make room for a new wood-frame double dwelling, 42 feet, six inches by 42 feet at its foundation. The old house was reportedly moved to become a private home nearby. The annual report of the Lighthouse Board announced that the lighthouse's watch room and the dwelling were connected by "speaking tubes." Along with the new house, a small brick oil house was added to store the station's kerosene.

The light was extinguished from April to July 1898 during the Spanish-American War, out of fear that it would serve to guide enemy vessels into Portland Harbor. The fortifications that had been established adjacent to the light station in 1872 were enlarged around this time.

Anyone passing through the grounds during this period had to explain his or her presence to a sentry. Once, when he was returning to the lighthouse, Joshua Strout was stopped by the sentry, who didn't recognize the old man. "Where do you want to go?" he asked. Strout replied, "Well, I was thinking of going down to the light." When asked if he knew someone there, the keeper responded, "I guess maybe I know the lighthouse keeper. I've brought up his family there for about 35 years."

The year 1900 saw a major repointing of the tower; many of the original stones were replaced. In the same year, two new oil engines with air compressors replaced the old fog signal equipment. Five hundred feet of piping installed around the same time connected the station to the public water supply.

This photo, taken in 1890 shows lumber that was used in the building of the new 1891 keeper's house. (courtesy of the Cape Elizabeth Historical Preservation Society)

Shortly after the keeper's house was rebuilt in 1891. (from the collection of the author)

An early version of the *Annie C. Maguire* inscription on a rock near the lighthouse
(courtesy of the Museum at Portland Head Light)

The *Annie C. Maguire* inscription as it looked in March 2017 (photo by the author)

In September 1903, the Strouts were warned before the first practice firing of new 10-inch guns a short distance away at Fort Williams. Framed pictures were taken off the walls in the keeper's house, and everything breakable was wrapped in cloth and placed in the middle of the rooms. The lighthouse's lens was wrapped in six thicknesses of bed quilts. When the guns were fired, many of the windows in the keeper's house were shattered, and plaster fell from the ceilings in white clouds.

When Joshua Strout retired at 77 in 1904, his son Joseph Woodbury Strout became the next principal keeper. He remained in the position until 1928, ending 59 years of the family at Portland Head.

Joseph Strout's son, John A. Strout, born in 1891, continued the family tradition by serving as an assistant keeper. It was John A. Strout who first painted the words memorializing the 1886 *Annie C. Maguire* wreck on a rock near the lighthouse on the day he assumed his duties as assistant keeper in January 1912. He had to chip away some of the rock to make a flat surface before he could paint.

John A. Strout's son, John, wrote in *Lighthouse Digest* that his father recalled as a boy of seven hearing the whistle salute of the steamer *Portland* as it passed. The *Portland* sank in a tremendous snowstorm in November 1898, and around 200 lives were lost. At Portland Head, the foghorn sounded for 72 straight hours during the storm.

In his book *Lighthouses of the Maine Coast*, Robert T. Sterling described a wreck that occurred in the summer of 1914. A steamship was returning to Portland from Boston in fog that was "thick as mud." The vessel ran up on the rocks not far from the lighthouse, and its distress whistles could be heard for miles. A lifesaving crew from Cape Elizabeth, with the help of the revenue cutter *Androscoggin*, was able to haul the steamer off the rocks at high tide. Some of the passengers were removed immediately, but some remained aboard until the ship was refloated, getting a "great thrill" from the experience, according to Sterling.

Around 1900 (U.S. Coast Guard photo)

The U.S. Lighthouse Service Bulletin of September 1, 1916, related that "windows were forced out, finish ripped off, roof torn open" by the practice firing of large guns at Fort Williams, and it also reported "injury to the brickwork of the three chimneys of the double dwelling."

On one occasion, two of the chimneys were completely severed at the bottom. Casings were subsequently installed to protect the chimneys. It was later reported that firing of the guns in 1917 resulted in many broken panes of glass in the lighthouse lantern.

PORTLAND HEAD LIGHT
Portland, Me.

# Safety!

THE keeper of the light must have one purpose always in mind.

Whatever befalls in his long vigil, he must keep his light burning.

Ships watch for it. Thousands upon thousands of lives depend upon it. Whether the sea be calm or stormy the lighthouse has come to mean safety, and the keeper's duty is to guard that safety.

Every one in the organization of S. W. STRAUS & Co. realizes today that the Straus record of Forty-one Years Without Loss To Any Investor has become a beacon of safety for investors all around the world. Each member of this organization is a guardian of that safety. All have a common purpose—to keep this beacon ever burning.

IF you are interested in investment safety, and desire good bonds yielding 6 and 6½% interest, that will be paid in cash on the days due, investigate the securities we offer, in $1000, $500, and $100 denominations. As a first step, we suggest that you call or write for

BOOKLET L-30

## S.W. STRAUS & CO.

ESTABLISHED 1882  ·  OFFICES IN FORTY CITIES  ·  INCORPORATED

CHICAGO—*Straus Building*  NEW YORK—*Straus Building*
CLARK AND MADISON STREETS  FIFTH AVE. AT 46TH STREET

## 41 YEARS WITHOUT LOSS TO ANY INVESTOR

© 1923—S. W. S. & Co., Inc.

A 1923 newspaper ad (from the collection of the author)

# 1928 to Automation (1989)

John W. Cameron, an assistant keeper beginning in 1904, took over as principal keeper when Joseph Strout retired in 1928. The light was converted from kerosene to electricity around the same time, and Cameron later commented that the change was a welcome one, as it "relieved the keepers of the chore of 'lighting up' each night." The characteristic of the light was changed at this time from fixed to a sequence of two seconds on, two seconds off.

When John Cameron retired in 1929, Frank O. Hilt became principal keeper. Another notable wreck occurred on October 4, 1932, a little past 6:00 p.m., when the fishing schooner *Lochinvar* ran aground on the rocks just about 100 feet from where the *Annie C. Maguire* had hit in 1886. There were 14 men on the schooner, which was carrying 40,000 pounds of haddock, when it struck the rocks in dense fog. The schooner sank within 15 minutes, but the men were able to escape to their dories, and there was

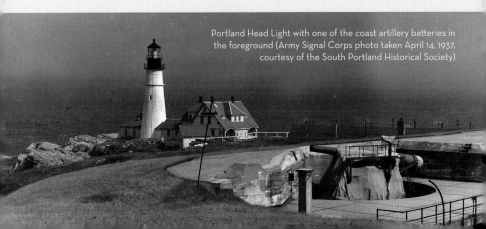

Portland Head Light with one of the coast artillery batteries in the foreground (Army Signal Corps photo taken April 14, 1937, courtesy of the South Portland Historical Society)

Circa 1912, Keeper Joseph Strout (second from left) with visitors (courtesy of the Cape Elizabeth Historical Preservation Society)

no loss of life. The upper parts of the masts could be seen above the water for several days.

1931 view of the *USS Constitution* passing the lighthouse (from the collection of the author)

A month later, on November 10, 1932, a tremendous storm with winds topping 60 miles per hour sent waves over the station's buildings, tearing boards and shingles from the fog signal building and briefly stopping the operation of the fog signal.

Circa 1931 photo by Ralph T. Blood (Library of Congress)

The station got a new fog signal during Hilt's tenure in 1938, when a three-horn diaphragm chime horn system replaced the old Daboll trumpet.

(photo by the author)

A new fog signal was installed in 1938
(U.S. Coast Guard photo)

The new signal included a large horn aimed toward Halfway Rock and two smaller horns facing Portland Harbor and the Portland Lightship.

On July 1, 1939, the civilian Lighthouse Service was merged with the U.S. Coast Guard. Since 1910, management had been with the Bureau of Lighthouses under the Department of Commerce. With the change in 1939, civilian lighthouse keepers were given the choice of remaining civilian until retirement or joining the Coast Guard.

Roughly half chose to join the Coast Guard. Portland Head Light retained civilian keepers as late as 1956, at times serving alongside Coast Guard keepers.

Robert Thayer Sterling, a journalist who wrote the book *Lighthouses of the Maine Coast and the Men Who Keep Them* in 1935, became the principal keeper in 1944. The light was dark for three years during World War II, from June 1942 to June 1945.

The light station was off-limits to

The fog signal was installed in 1938. The center and largest horn pointed toward Halfway Rock Lighthouse. Two smaller horns were directed toward the Portland Lightship and Portland Harbor. (National Archives)

Portland, Maine, Portland Head Light.

74:—PORTLAND HEAD LIGHT AT NIGHT, PORTLAND, ME.

PORTLAND, ME., PORTLAND HEAD LIGHT AT NIGHT

66367

PORTLAND HEAD LIGHT, CASCO BAY, PORTLAND, MAINE. OLDEST LIGHTHOUSE ON THE COAST.
FIRST KEEPER APPOINTED IN 1791 BY GEORGE WASHINGTON    4321

Moonlight on the Portland Headlight, Cape Elizabeth, Maine — D-12

(from the collection of the author)

# LOSS OF THE EAGLE 56

Visitors to Portland Head Light, as they walk along the fence to the south of the lighthouse, encounter a somber plaque memorializing the loss of the *Eagle 56* in 1945, a disaster that produced the largest loss of life in New England during World War II.

The *Eagle 56*, a World War 1–era sub chaser, arrived at its final port at Portland, Maine, in the summer of 1944. At Portland, the primary job of the crew of the *Eagle 56* was to tow a target float off of Cape Elizabeth, so that U.S. Navy and Marine bomber pilots could practice their aim before leaving for the Pacific.

A little past noon on April 23, a German U-boat, the *U-853*, drew within 600 yards of the *Eagle 56* as it sat at a dead stop about three miles offshore. A torpedo fired by the *U-853* ran swiftly into the *Eagle 56*. The boat was ripped in half, and the resulting geyser of water was reported to be at least 200 feet high. The explosion was seen as far away as Portland Head Lighthouse and was heard by residents of Portland.

All the men on the bridge and almost all the men below deck in the bow section were killed. Most of the survivors were suffering from hypothermia by the time they were pulled from the ocean by the crew of the destroyer *USS Selfridge* almost 20 minutes after the explosion. Only 13 men aboard the *Eagle 56* escaped with their lives, and 49 men died.

The SS *Black Point*, a collier cruising along the Rhode Island coast on the morning of May 5, was sunk by a torpedo fired by the *U-853*. The *Black Point* sank in 15 minutes, taking with it the lives of 12 men. Near midnight that night, U.S. Navy

(photo by the author)

and Coast Guard vessels located the *U-853* using sonar. Depth charges were dropped, but the U-boat continued moving. The bombardment continued through the night, and two Navy blimps deployed rocket bombs that broke the submarine's hull. The next morning, a diver confirmed that the U-boat had been sunk. Six hours after the sinking, German forces in Europe surrendered.

The original pronouncement on the *Eagle 56* disaster stated that it was caused by a boiler explosion. In the fall of 2000, the Naval Historical Center agreed to re-examine the case. After a few months, senior archivist Bernard Cavalcante determined that the *Eagle 56* had been sunk "by enemy action," and recommended that the survivors be awarded the Purple Heart. In late 2001, the secretary of the Navy concurred.

On June 8, 2002, at 10:00 a.m., a ceremony was held aboard the *USS Salem* in Quincy, Massachusetts. Relatives of the *Eagle 56* crew from around the country attended, along with the three remaining survivors: Harold Petersen, Johnny Breeze, and John Scagnelli. Purple Heart medals were awarded to the men, and posthumous medals were presented to relatives of the other crewmembers.

Aerial photo of Fort Williams, circa World War II, with barracks and other buildings is shown. Portland Head Light is visible at the upper left. (courtesy of the South Portland Historical Society)

This photo was taken in 1955 by Richard B. Innes just after the lighthouse tower had been sandblasted in preparation for repainting. (courtesy of the Museum at Portland Head Light)

unauthorized visitors for much of the war. During that period, additional barracks and other buildings were added to Fort Williams. Practice firings of the fort's guns in the World War II period caused the heavy iron stove in the keeper's house kitchen to vibrate, according to Sterling.

After the war, a constant stream of tourists was once again a way of life at Portland Head. Under the station's first Coast Guard keeper, William Lockhart, the station was open to the public Monday through Friday from 10:00 a.m. to 3:00 p.m., except when the fog signal was sounding.

There was little privacy for keepers and their families. Wes Gamage, a Coast Guard keeper in the early 1960s, was always careful to keep the doors and first-floor windows locked so tourists couldn't wander in. Once,

Circa 1948 (U.S. Coast Guard photo)

A 1952 view (photo courtesy of Dolly Bicknell)

Circa 1960s—notice the Christmas tree (courtesy of the Museum at Portland Head Light)

feet of steel fence out of concrete, and left the house a "foot deep in mud and flotsam, including starfish." A wave had broken a window in the house 25 feet above the ground. Allen said that the winds during the storm reached 92 miles per hour.

The Coast Guard keepers and their families were evacuated during a storm in March 1977. The power lines were downed, and the generator failed after waves broke open drums of diesel fuel, leaving the lighthouse dark for the first time since World War II.

A rededication event took place at the lighthouse on July 4, 1985, with Vice President George H. W. Bush presiding. Senator William Cohen

Gamage's wife was taking a bath upstairs when several camera-toting tourists suddenly burst right into the bathroom. It turned out she had forgotten to lock one of the doors.

Severe weather has continued to plague the station in recent decades. In February 1972, Coast Guardsman Robert Allen reported to the *Maine Sunday Telegram* that a storm had torn the fog bell from its house, ripped 80

Chimney repairs in 1965
(from the collection of the author)

At the August 7, 1989, celebration. (photos by the author)

and Governor Joseph E. Brennan were among the special guests. Vice President Bush arrived in his speedboat from his summer home in Kennebunkport. "If you saw us come in that boat, you can understand why I appreciate this light," he said. "I need all the navigational help I can get, believe me, going around in these waters."

By late 1985, all but 32 light stations in the First Coast Guard District, which includes Maine, had been automated and destaffed. By late 1987 the number was down to 16, and Portland Head was slated to be one of the last to make the transition.

On August 7, 1989, a celebration was held at Portland Head commemorating the 200th anniversary of the creation of a federal lighthouse service. The day also marked the automation of Portland Head Light and the transfer of the last two Coast Guard keepers, Davis Simpson and Nathan Wasserstrom, as

(photo by the author)

well as the leasing of the light station property (except the tower) to the town of Cape Elizabeth.

With approximately 600 people in attendance at the celebration, Maine's Senator George Mitchell, Congressman Joseph Brennan, and the lighthouse historian F. Ross Holland spoke while the Nantucket Lightship paraded offshore with a flotilla of Coast Guard vessels. In his keynote address, Holland said:

*Americans love lighthouses. Artists and photographers find them picturesque. The dreamer finds them romantic. The boaters find them comforting.*

*The navigator finds them helpful. The shore walker finds them peaceful. The historic preservationist feels they make a statement about a period of time. The historian is fascinated by the human and technological stories they embody. And the idealist is drawn to them because they symbolize man's humanity to man.*

Rear Admiral Richard Rybacki, the Coast Guard's First District commander, said in his address to the crowd: "I can think of nothing more noble. The lighthouse symbolizes all that is good in mankind. We are not here to celebrate an ending. We are here to immortalize a tradition."

The *Nantucket Lightship (LV 112)* was nearby as part of the August 7, 1989, celebration (photo by the author)

(photo by John Whalen)

# Keepers of the Light

This chapter contains a list and brief biographies of all the known keepers and assistant keepers at Portland Head Light from the light's inception to the present day.

## Civilian Principal Keepers

Joseph K. Greenleaf (1791–1795); Reuben Freeman (1795–1796); Barzillai Delano (1796–1820); Joshua Freeman (1820–1840); Richard Lee (1840–1849); John F. Watts (1849–1853); John W. Coolidge (1853–1854); James S. Williams (1854); James Delano (1854–1861); Elder M. Jordan (1861–1869); Joshua F. Strout (1869–1904); Joseph W. Strout (1904–1928); John W. Cameron (1928–1929); Frank. O. Hilt (1929–1944); Robert Thayer Sterling (1944–1946); William T. Burns (1954–1956)

## Civilian Assistant Keepers

Mary Strout (1869–1877); Joseph W. Strout (1877–1904); Gil Strout (ca. 1880s); John W. Cameron 1904–1928); John A. Strout (1912–1915); Millard Urquhart (1928); Robert Thayer Sterling (1928–1944); William T. Burns (ca. 1944–1954)

## Coast Guard Keepers

William L. Lockhart (1946–1950); William F. Yost (1950); Howard Beebe (1950–1951); Earle E. Benson (1952–1954); Edward Frank (1956); Archie McLaughlin (1956–1957); Henry E. Leonard (1957–1960); Weston E. Gamage Jr. (1960–1962); Armand Houde (1962–1965); Walter Dodge (1963); Thomas Reed (1966–1967); Franklin D. Allen (1968–1974); Kenneth A. Perry (ca. 1973); Roy Cavanaugh (1974–1977); Anthony Di

Part of a 1792 letter from Joseph Greenleaf (National Archives)

## Joseph Greenleaf

(1791–1795)

Captain Joseph Greenleaf, a 51-year-old native of Portland and a veteran of the American Revolution, was approved by President George Washington to be the first keeper at Portland Head. Greenleaf and his wife, Susanna (Pearson), had six children, but two had died and one had already married when the family moved into the keeper's house.

At first, Greenleaf received no salary as keeper; his payment was the right to live in the keeper's house, to farm the land, and to fish in the surrounding waters. As early as November 1791, Greenleaf wrote that he couldn't afford to remain keeper without financial compensation. Benjamin Lincoln, the local lighthouse superintendent, championed Greenleaf's cause, writing that the keeper's compensation was "below the rate at which he can afford to perform his service." The pleas fell on deaf ears in the Treasury Department.

In a June 1792 letter, Greenleaf complained of many hardships. During the previous winter, he wrote, the ice on the lantern glass was often so thick that he had to melt it off with a flame.

(photo by the author)

(photo by the author)

He placed an ad in a local newspaper on December 24, 1792, that seems to indicate that area merchants had donated funds to the keeper:

*The Subscriber, Keeper of the Light house at the entrance of this harbour, embraces the present opportunity to acknowledge the obligations which he feels himself under to the merchants and other gentlemen of the town of Portland, for the generous subscription which they have lately made towards the relief of himself and his family. They may be assured, that as Keeper of said Light house, no exertions shall be wanting on his part, for the promotion of their interest and the preservation of their property.*

In July 1793, Greenleaf was granted an annual salary of $160, approved by President Washington. Not much more than two years later, Greenleaf died of an apparent stroke while in his boat in Portland Harbor on October 3, 1795. He was 56 years old. The *Eastern Herald* reported:

*On Saturday morning last, died very suddenly, Capt. Joseph Greenleaf of Cape*

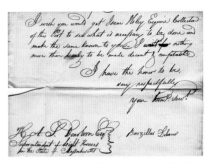

Part of a June 1814 letter from Keeper Barzillai Delano (National Archives)

*Elizabeth. He had crossed the [Fore] river in a boat alone, and on coming ashore observed, that he never had before worried himself so much at the oar. After doing some business in town, he stepped on board his boat to return; but it was observed by some standing on the wharf, as he began to row, that he suddenly fell down in his boat. Assistance went to him immediately; but no sign of life was discoverable. Capt. Greenleaf had been keeper of the light-house on Portland-point, from the time of its establishment to his death, in which office he faithfully discharged his duty, to the satisfaction of those "who occupy their business on great waters." His death is not only a loss to his sorrowful wife and children; but will be sincerely regretted by all his acquaintances.*

Greenleaf was buried at the Eastern Cemetery in Portland.

## Barzillai Delano
(1796–1820)

Barzillai Delano was appointed keeper in early March 1796. Delano, born in Falmouth, Maine, in 1745, was a blacksmith who had lobbied for the appointment when the lighthouse was first built. He had been recommended to be the first keeper by the local customs collector, Benjamin Lincoln.

Delano's first wife, Mary (Cobb), with whom he had six children, died in 1783. He had married his second wife, Hanna (Dyer), in 1784, and they had one son.

Delano's salary as keeper of $225 yearly was raised to $300 in 1812, after a petition with 22 signatures was submitted in his behalf. The petitioners stated that Delano had "discharged his trust most faithfully" and that a salary of $300 would "be but a bare subsistence for a small family."

Delano wrote to the local lighthouse superintendent in June 1814, complaining that the keeper's house was in need of "considerable repairs to make it comfortable." The house had no cellar, and Delano asked for a "small porch" with a cellar to be added to the house. Delano got more than he asked for, as the keeper's house was entirely rebuilt in 1816.

Barzillai Delano died in June 1820, at the age of 75; he is buried at the Mount Pleasant Cemetery in South Portland. (His name on the gravestone is spelled "Barzilla.") His grandson, James, later served as keeper from 1854 to 1861.

## Joshua Freeman
(1820–1840)

Joshua Freeman was born in Falmouth, Maine, in 1763. His father, also named Joshua Freeman, had served as a lieutenant in the 7th Massachusetts Regiment in the capture of the French fortress at Louisbourg, Nova Scotia, in

# THE HOSPITALITY OF JOSHUA FREEMAN

## AN 1825 ARTICLE IN THE EASTERN ARGUS DESCRIBED
## THE PLEASURES OF A VISIT TO PORTLAND HEAD:

*I know of no excursion as pleasant as a jaunt to the Light House. There our friend Freeman is always at home, and ready to serve you. There you can angle in safety and comfort for the cunning cunner, while old ocean is rolling majestically at your feet, and when wearied and fatigued with this amusement, you will find a pleasant relaxation in tumbling the huge rocks from the brinks of the steep and rocky precipices. . . . I know of no equal to a ride or sail to the Light House and earnestly recommend it to all poor devils who, like myself, are afflicted with the dyspepsia, gout, or any of the diseases to which human flesh is heir.*

1745, and later worked as an innkeeper and tea merchant in Falmouth. Nothing is known of the younger Joshua's career before he became a lighthouse keeper, but it seems likely that he was involved with his father's businesses.

Freeman had a housekeeper, Jane Dyer, who was 16 years old when she went to work for him around 1821 at a salary of 50 cents per week. She later married Daniel Strout, a storekeeper from a prominent local family, and they had seven children. Their oldest son, Joshua Freeman Strout, who was named for Joshua Freeman when he was born in 1826, went on to be one of the longest-serving keepers at Portland Head.

Joshua Freeman Strout's son, Joseph Strout, later spoke about his father's namesake in an interview: "Old Cap'n Freeman used to sit in a big arm chair with a coil of rope near him so if a shipwreck came sudden he would be prepared."

Joseph Strout also said that his grandmother pointed out a cupboard in the keeper's house kitchen where Joshua Freeman kept his rum. "He used to sell it for three cents a glass for people who came out here and fished," said Joseph Strout. "The best was kept for the minister, of course."

A local newspaper asked in 1825, "Are you fond of cool punch, London particular, old cognac, and a hundred etceteras, no man is better provided with these articles than Captain Freeman."

Freeman's wife, Eliza, died in October 1830. Freeman was still serving as keeper when he died at the age of 76 on January 2, 1840. Joshua and Eliza Freeman are buried in Portland's Eastern Cemetery.

## Richard Lee
### (1840–1849)

Richard Lee became keeper in April 1840, three months after the death of Joshua Freeman, at a yearly salary of $350. Lee wrote a letter in August 1842 for I. W. P. Lewis's report to Congress, and it painted a dire picture: "The lighthouse tower appears to me to have been built very badly at first; the mortar in the walls seeming to be all sand, and no lime. I am not allowed any boat; and I hire the adjacent land for pasturage, the Government estate here being so small that there is barely room for a garden."

Later in 1843, Lee retracted his statement, as did several other keepers who had been quite critical in Lewis's report. The tower was "strong and tight," he said, and would probably remain a "good tower for hundreds of years." It isn't clear whether Lee had been pressured to change his statement or if he feared he might lose his job.

## John F. Watts
### (1849–1853)

John F. Watts, a Maine native who was born about 1800, worked as a mariner and shipmaster before his lighthouse-keeping years. He and his wife, Olive (Morton), had 11 children, at least seven of whom died before the age of six. Olive died at the age of 45, and Watts married Eliza (Small) in 1844.

An 1851 report by the newly commissioned U.S. Lighthouse Board stated that because Watts was poorly trained and had received no written instructions on the operation of the light, he was forced to hire a man to instruct him for two days. Instead of

*Portland Light, Entrance Portland Harbor, Me.*

*Portland, Me.   Portland Head Light.*

PUB. BY C. S. WOOLWORTH & CO.

Portland Light, Cape Elizabeth, Me.

(from the collection of the author)

(photo by the author)

proper scissors for trimming the wicks in the oil lamps, he was using "common seamstress scissors."

Watts died in Lynn, Massachusetts, in May 1874. He is buried in the Forest Hill Cemetery in Cape Elizabeth.

## James Delano
### (1854–1861)

James Delano, born in Cape Elizabeth in 1812, was the grandson of the earlier keeper, Barzillai Delano. He and his wife, Harriet (Lane), had two children. According to William O. Thomson's book *Portland Head Light: A Place in History*, Delano was once forced to strike the fog bell with a wooden mallet during one foggy period when the striking machinery malfunctioned. James Delano died in 1878 in Portland.

## Elder M. Jordan
### (1861–1869)

Elder Jordan was born in Cape Elizabeth in 1813, and he and his wife Eliza (Staples) had four children, including a daughter born around the time he became keeper at Portland Head. Jordan was at Portland Head for a number of significant events, including the 1863 Confederate raid in Portland Harbor, the 1864 shipwreck of the steamer *Bohemian*, the subsequent increase of the lighthouse tower's height by 20 feet, and the installation of a powerful second-order Fresnel lens. Elder Jordan resigned as keeper in 1869 and died in September 1880.

## Joshua Freeman Strout
### (1869–1904)

Joshua Freeman Strout was born in Portland on August 13, 1826. His mother, Jane (Dyer) Strout, had worked as a housekeeper at Portland Head for Joshua Freeman in the 1820s. She married Daniel Strout, and Daniel and Jane named their first son after Keeper Joshua Freeman.

Circa 1891. (U.S. Coast Guard photo)

Joshua was one of six children. His brother Daniel was a carpenter who built many houses in the Cape Elizabeth area and later ran a grocery store. Another brother, Willis, served as town auditor and selectman in Cape Elizabeth.

Strout went to sea at the age of 11 and served as the cook on a tugboat by the time he was 18. He first served as captain on the maiden voyage of the brig *Scotland*, built at Benjamin W. Pickett's shipyard in South Portland. He also owned the *Scotland* and sailed it for two years as far as Cuba and South America. He captained several more schooners and brigs in the ensuing years, and was said to have transported many "Forty-Niners" to San Francisco during the gold rush.

While he was captain of the brig *Andres*, Strout suffered a severe fall from the masthead. The injuries he sustained forced him to give up his life at sea in exchange for the somewhat more tranquil life of a lighthouse keeper. He became keeper at Portland Head Light in 1869 at a salary of $620 per year, after the previous keeper, Elder Jordan, had resigned.

Joshua Freeman Strout. (courtesy of the Cape Elizabeth Historical Preservation Society)

Strout's wife, Mary (Berry), a native of Pownal, Maine, was named an assistant keeper at a salary of $480 per year. She held the position until 1877, when her son Joseph took on the title of assistant keeper. Joshua and Mary Strout had 11 children. Three of their sons—Stephen (in 1879), Charles (in 1882), and John (in 1890)—were all lost at sea during the family's years at Portland Head. A daughter, Jane, also died in 1890; according to some sources, she was on the *Charles Haskell* with her brother John when it sank. Another of Joshua and Mary's sons died in infancy. Two other sons, Joseph and Gilman, served as assistants to their father.

Joshua and Mary's daughter Susan was born in the old keeper's house in 1871, and she was married to Edwin Field in 1898 in the parlor of the 1891 house. She told a reporter in 1947 that she could recall the crowds that came to see the wreck of the *Annie C. Maguire* in

## BILLY THE PARROT

An African parrot named Billy was a well-known member of the Strout household for many years beginning in 1887 when he was presented to Joshua Strout. Billy heard the keepers in times of poor visibility call to each other, "Fog coming in; blow the horn!" One day, when a sudden fog enveloped the station but nobody noticed, Billy cried out, "Fog coming in; blow the horn!" Billy became an avid fan of radio in his declining years and was said to be nearly 90 years old when he died in 1942.

(photo by the author)

1886, and she remembered the keepers being hoisted in baskets to whitewash the tower each year. Another memory was tourists catching fish near the lighthouse and cooking them on the surrounding rocks.

In an 1898 interview, Joshua Strout said that he had gone as long as 17 years at a stretch without taking time off and as long as two years without going as far as Portland. Strout, the oldest keeper on the Maine coast at the time, retired in May 1904. He died at the age of 80 on March 10, 1907, and was survived by his wife of 56 years. He is buried in the Mount Pleasant Cemetery in South Portland. His widow died in 1913.

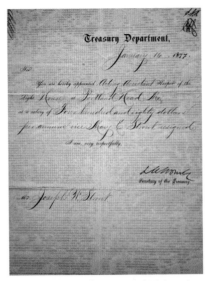

An 1877 letter confirming Joseph W. Strout's appointment as an assistant keeper (courtesy of the Museum at Portland Head Light)

## Joseph Woodbury Strout
(assistant 1877–1904, principal keeper 1904–1928)

Joshua Freeman Strout's son Joseph Woodbury Strout was born in Cape Elizabeth in 1859. He and his wife, Mary (Eagon), had four children—two sons, Charles and John, and two daughters, Martha and Amelia. Their son John A. Strout became an assistant

Joseph Woodbury Strout (courtesy of the Museum at Portland Head Light)

Joseph Strout, circa 1920s (from the collection of the author)

keeper under his father in 1912 and later served at Graves Light, Boston Light, and Dumpling Rock Light in Massachusetts.

Joseph W. Strout was described in a newspaper article as a "bronzed, hardy little man, comfortably inclined to corpulence," with "kindly eyes." He was an assistant keeper under his father beginning in 1877, when he was 18 years old, and he succeeded his father as principal keeper in 1904. In 1910, he was quoted in the *Lewiston Journal*: "We've all got the lighthouse fever in our blood. . . . Father was keeper before me. Joshua Freeman Strout, that was his name, and a fine old man he was, too. He was named for Captain Joshua Freeman. He kept the light, too, Captain Freeman did, in the days when they burned whale oil and had 16 lamps."

In a 1978 article in *Down East* magazine, Arthur Cameron, son of assistant keeper John Cameron, wrote about accompanying Joseph Strout to the lantern to "light up."

*Between the floor of the deck and the dome overhead were long steel-ribbed windows covered on the inside with yellow curtains to protect the lens from the sun. Keeper Strout instructed me that my job was to take down these curtains by means of a hooked pole and to fold them carefully. On the way down the tower I was to place them in a cabinet on the first deck so that they would be handy to hang up again in the morning after the light had been extinguished.*

In his book *Lighthouses of the Maine Coast and the Men Who Keep Them*, Robert Thayer Sterling called Joseph Strout "one of the most popular lightkeepers of his day or any yet to come. His genial disposition, his hearty laugh, together with his good stories of the sea, won him the admiration of all who met him." Sterling also wrote that Strout was "a very pleasant person to meet," and that "his stories were as salty as his appearance."

Joseph Strout was known as "Cap'n Joe" to many friends and visitors to Portland Head. Every Christmas, he received many gifts from people who had visited the lighthouse, in gratitude for his kind hospitality. He remained at the station until he retired in 1928, ending 59 years of the family at Portland Head. He had lived at the lighthouse from the age of 10 to the age of 69.

Robert T. Sterling, who served as an assistant keeper under Joseph Strout and later authored the aforementioned book on Maine lighthouses, wrote that when Strout retired, "the summer guests lost a very beloved man." Joseph Strout died in December 1931, after a long illness.

# The Strout Family Album

(photos courtesy of the Museum at Portland Head Light)

oshua Strout's sons Charles (center) and ohn (right), with a friend. Charles and John ere both lost at sea.

Mary Strout, wife of Joseph Woodbury Strout, and their daughter Martha in 1883.

oshua F. Strout's wife Mary Berry Strout and their granddaughter Martha in )5, outside the family's house in Cape Elizabeth. The house was built in 1789.

Joseph W. Strout and his
flower garden, circa 1920s.

Joseph W. Strout,
circa 1920s.

Joseph W. Strout sharing a donut with a visitor, circa 1920s.

Circa 1920s.

Joseph W. Strout circa 1920s.

Joseph W. Strout with a riding instructor from Fort Williams, circa 1920s.

Joseph W. Strout and his wife Mary are on the right side of this photo, posing with some visitors to the lighthouse, circa 1920s.

Joseph W. Strout in August 1924. The person seen in the window might have been his wife, Mary.

Mary Eagon Strout, wife of Joseph W. Strout, with grandson John A. Strout Jr.

John A. "Jack" Strout next to the Fresnel lens at Portland Head Light in 1952.

During a visit of some Strout family descendants around 1970, Donna Strout (left) became the fifth generation of Strouts to climb the lighthouse stairs.

# John W. Cameron

(assistant 1904–1928, principal keeper
1928–1929)

John W. Cameron was born in
Southport, Maine, in 1859, the same
year Joseph Strout was born. He
married Harriet "Hattie" Bonney.
Cameron's career in the Lighthouse
Service began when he spent three
years as a crewman on the lighthouse
tender *Lilac*. He was eventually
assigned as a third assistant keeper at
the Cape Elizabeth Two Lights station,
followed by two years (1902–04) as a
first assistant keeper at Spring Point
Ledge Light in South Portland.

John W. Cameron (courtesy of the South
Portland Historical Society)

Harriett "Hattie" Cameron (courtesy of the South
Portland Historical Society)

Cameron transferred to Portland
Head as an assistant keeper beginning
in 1904. According to an article by his
son, Arthur Cameron, John appeared
in a 1911 silent movie called *The Spirit
of the Light*, or *Love Watches on Through
the Years*. A lighthouse keeper and his
daughter were central characters, and
Cameron played the role of an assistant
keeper, appropriately enough. His
daughter later said, "Pa needed no
makeup, as he had a healthy tan, but
the director insisted in dressing him
up to look like an old sea dog." Sadly,
it appears that no prints of the movie
have survived.

Cameron listed the keeper's duties in a report in October 1928:

• *Care and operation of a 2nd-order incandescent electric light.*

• *Care and operation of a compressed air fog signal.*

• *Cleaning and minor repair of above apparatus.*

• *Cleaning, painting, and making minor repairs to structures.*

• *Care and attention of grounds of station.*

• *Keeping station records and preparing and submitting periodical reports.*

• *Observing weather conditions and aids to navigation.*

Cameron then elaborated:

• *The work of Keeper at an important station as this, where shipping is conducted during day and night requires most one's time and attention. As this station marks the entrance to Portland Harbor, it is very essential that this place be kept up to the standard continually.*

• *Care of the light and tower occupies the best part of the morning hours of the day.*

*The afternoons are taken up in doing the preliminary work around the station and grounds.*

*For a station like this where there are only two men, the watches can only be so arranged that one man during the afternoon can be on the station work, as the keeper who takes the first watch must have the required amount of rest to perform his work faithfully.*

• *The work about the Fog Signal, in the upkeep of the machinery, occupies a great deal of one's time during the day, especially when it is in operation. . . .*

• *The responsibility for the safe upkeep of the station and property falls upon the Principal Keeper as a part of his duties each hour of the day and night.*

*During the vacation season much of the Keeper's time is required at this station in entertaining the large number of Summer Vacationists, that are always greatly interest[ed] in this place as it is one of the first built during the Administration of President George Washington's time. . . .*

• *Being located as it is next to the grounds of a fortification (Fort Williams) where there is target practicing going on each year causes much damage to the station as a whole by the great concussion.*

Robert T. Sterling, who worked with Cameron as an assistant keeper, later wrote that Cameron was often asked how he tolerated Maine winters. Cameron's answer was, "Nobody living in New England during severe winters could brag about being warm."

Cameron took over as principal keeper when Joseph Strout retired in 1928. His tenure as principal keeper was brief, as he reached the mandatory retirement age of 70 in 1929. He died on October 31, 1949, and is buried in the Evergreen Cemetery in Portland.

Cameron's son, Arthur, wrote a short novel called *The Lighthouse at Portland Head*. The story featured the adventures of a fictional keeper, Zebadiah Prout, based on Joshua Strout. The novel featured a talking parrot, lots of colorful characters, and even a sea monster.

## Frank O. Hilt
### (1929–1944)

When Cameron retired in 1929, Frank O. Hilt became principal keeper. Hilt, who was born in St. George, Maine, in 1879, went to sea at a young age and eventually became the captain of the schooner *Mary Langdon* and other vessels. Hilt married Adora (Robinson) in 1906, and they had one son, Willard.

Frank Hilt on his giant checkerboard with Anna-Myrle Snow, wife of historian Edward Rowe Snow. (photo by Edward Rowe Snow, courtesy of Dolly Bicknell)

Beginning in 1913, Hilt served as an assistant keeper and later principal keeper at the isolated light station at Matinicus Rock. While at Matinicus Rock, Hilt doubled as a warden for the Audubon Society; an estimated 18,000 common and Arctic terns were nesting there at the time.

Hilt was in charge at Portland Head when the order came to turn off

Frank O. Hilt (courtesy of James W. Claflin)

## THE DOGGY DOCTOR

Sue, a chow dog, lived at Portland Head Light with Keeper Frank Hilt and his wife for some years. One of Sue's puppies, Chang, was adopted by Assistant Keeper Robert T. Sterling. One day, it appeared that Chang had a toothache—he'd whimper and yelp every time he bit anything hard.

With his mother nearby, Chang yelped with pain while he was gnawing a bone. Sue came over to her puppy, rolled him onto his back, and stuck her snout into his mouth. Chang let out a loud cry as Sue dropped the extracted tooth onto the grass. Chang had no further dental problems.

A while later, Chang got a fishhook stuck through his upper lip. Hilt was able to remove the hook safely, but Sue proceeded to lick her pup in the injured area vigorously several times a day for a week, until the wound was healed. A veterinarian commented that Sue's doctoring had prevented infection.

If you visited with the keepers at Portland Head Light in the World War II years, you were likely treated to the amazing stories of Sue, the doggy doctor.

the light in October 1942 as part of a coastal blackout during World War II. The fog signal remained in operation during the blackout; the light was reinstated in June 1945.

Hilt remained principal keeper at Portland Head until 1944. One of his more unusual accomplishments was the construction of a giant checkerboard near the base of the lighthouse tower. Edward Rowe Snow, in his book *The Romance of Casco Bay*, wrote that one of his most delightful memories of Portland Head was photographing Hilt contemplating a move on the giant board during a checkers match with Snow's wife, Anna-Myrle. Hilt "in his prime was a 300-pound giant," according to Snow.

Sue, the doggy doctor (courtesy of the Museum at Portland Head Light)

(photo by John Whalen)

PORTLAND HEAD LIGHT, CAPE ELIZABETH, ME.

CAPE ELIZABETH, ME.   Portland Head with an old sea running.        76

Robert Sterling and Frank Hilt (courtesy of the Maine Lighthouse Museum)

After his light-keeping years, Hilt was the captain of a vacation schooner, the *Lillian*, ported in Camden, Maine. According to his obituary, Hilt brought his schooner into the harbor and was then "stricken" while at a barbershop in Camden on August 12, 1949. He died en route to a hospital. He is buried in the North Parish Cemetery in Tenants Harbor, a village of St. George, Maine.

A 1940 photo taken by Robert Thayer Sterling
(from the collection of the author)

Robert T. Sterling with his dog, Chang (courtesy of James W. Claflin)

Robert Thayer Sterling (courtesy of the American Lighthouse Foundation)

## Robert T. Sterling

(assistant 1928–1944, principal keeper 1944–1946)

Robert Thayer Sterling, born at Peaks Island in Portland, Maine, in 1876, worked for several years as a young man in newspaper reporting for the *Portland Press*. He entered the Lighthouse Service in 1913 and spent time at Ram Island Ledge, Great Duck Island, Seguin Island, and Cape Elizabeth (Two Lights). A son, Robert Jr., was born while Sterling and his

wife, Martha, were stationed on Seguin Island.

Sterling arrived at Portland Head as an assistant in 1928. He wrote in a report that year: "An apprentice on entering the Lighthouse Service must first bear in mind that he is a 24-hour man—that is to say, his work is never done. Should conditions warrant his work the full 24 hours around, he could only look upon this task as that, for the good of the service."

Sterling moonlighted as a writer throughout his career, and he authored the substantial book *Lighthouses of the Maine Coast and the Men Who Keep Them* in 1935. A newspaper announcement informed readers that the book had been delayed because severe storms had slowed communications with lighthouse keepers. Sterling said he wasn't really in a hurry to finish the book, anyway, as his wife was anxious for its completion so he could paint the kitchen floor. In the book, Sterling declared Portland Head the most desirable of all light stations for keepers.

An interesting story of the Sterling years at Portland Head concerns the keeper's dog, Chang (sometimes spelled "Chiang"). Sterling claimed that Chang's grandfather was with

Circa 1948 (courtesy of the Cape Elizabeth Historical Preservation Society)

Admiral Byrd at the South Pole. Sterling's wife, Martha, liked to do her knitting in a favorite chair near a window. On one particular evening, Chang pawed at Martha's legs in a way that usually meant he wanted a drink of water. Moments after Martha went to the kitchen to get the water, a huge wave hit the house, breaking the window and sending shards of glass all over the chair. "Yes, sir," said Sterling, "that dog's got an instinct for the sea and what it may do to you." Sadly, Chang, who was photographed by many tourists, died in August 1939 when he was hit by a car while chasing another dog into the street.

Sterling succeeded Frank Hilt as principal keeper in 1944. He retired after 33 years as a lighthouse keeper in 1946. On the first day of his retirement, Sterling fell in his yard and broke a rib. As a result, he had to put his plans to attend some Boston Red Sox games on hold. Sterling died in 1958 and is buried at the Pond Grove Cemetery in Portland.

Portland Headlight, Portland, Maine                                    22

61196

Portland, Me. Portland Headlight from Water.

Portland Head.

## William L. Lockhart
(1946–1950)

The Coast Guard took over management of the lighthouses of the United States in 1939, but civilian lighthouse keepers were given the option of joining the Coast Guard or remaining civilians until retirement. Portland Head Light retained civilian keepers as late as 1956, and in some cases they served simultaneously with Coast Guard keepers. Boatswain's Mate First Class William Lockhart had previously been an assistant keeper at Great Duck Island and Rockland Breakwater.

William Lockhart was in charge during the memorable storm of March 4, 1947; he turned on an emergency generator and kept the light and fog signal going through the gale. Offshore near Cape Elizabeth, the collier *Oakey L. Alexander* split in two in high seas, and the crew was subsequently rescued via breeches buoy by the Coast Guard. Waves poured through the small space between the lighthouse tower and the fog signal building, eventually washing the old fog bell into the ocean. In spite of the damage done by the storm, Lockhart said the thundering surf provided an awesome spectacle. He watched a lone tug ride out the storm offshore, "bobbing about like a float," at times disappearing in the waves so that all that was visible was its mast.

In early September 1949, Lockhart spotted a huge, red ball of fire and a cloud of white smoke over the ocean, about 14 miles away. Lockhart said he had just taken some visitors to the top of the tower and saw the fireball

Circa 1946 (U.S. Coast Guard photo)

Circa 1949 (U.S. Coast Guard photo)

when he "happened to look southeast by south." There was speculation of a crashed plane or a boat fire, but an extensive search by the Coast Guard found nothing.

In 1949, Lockhart told a newspaper reporter, "Most of the folks who visit the reservation want to tour the lighthouse itself." When he had the time, Lockhart showed visitors up the spiral stairway, to the tune of about 200 people per week and as many as 56 in a day. There were no tower tours on foggy days, when Lockhart was too busy with the fog signal. But Lockhart enjoyed showing people around when

he could. "Everyone who comes to Portland still wants to see historic old Portland Head Light," he said.

Lockhart said that most visitors were more interested in enjoying the views than they were in the lighthouse's history. Most were thrilled with the scenery, but one woman from the Midwest expressed disappointment when she saw the Atlantic Ocean for the first time. "I thought it was bigger," she commented.

Lockhart and his wife moved to Southwest Harbor, Maine, after their years at Portland Head.

## William T. Burns

(assistant 1944–1954,
principal keeper 1954–1956)

William Burns was born in Eastbrook, Maine, in 1904. He came to Portland Head as a civilian assistant keeper in 1944, after time at Ram Island Ledge Light, the Portland Lightship, and Saddleback Ledge Light. He finished his career as Portland Head's last civilian keeper, sharing duty with Coast Guardsman Archie McLaughlin.

Burns was at the station for a tremendous storm on March 4, 1947. Waves washed away the fog bell, badly damaged the fog signal building, and left rocks and debris strewn all over the grounds.

Burns and his wife, Beatrice (Googins), were profiled in article in the *Portland Press Herald* in June 1956. At the time, Burns was working the night shift. After the end of his shift at 7:00 a.m., he had a cup of coffee and went to bed. The keepers alternated shifts, so Burns and his wife were always making adjustments, but Beatrice Burns said she liked having her husband home all the time. He kept busy in his spare time, constructing a model of the lighthouse and carving a lamp from driftwood. He also made wooden furniture, including a dresser and a handsome inlaid chess table. Beatrice enjoyed creating pretty lampshades.

Beatrice Burns taught school part-time, meaning clothes washing was

Former assistant keeper John A. Strout, left, with Keeper William T. Burns, right, in 1955 (courtesy of the Museum at Portland Head Light)

usually done on Saturdays. On nice days, the clothes were hung outside to dry, but Mrs. Burns complained at the time of the article that it had been raining every Saturday for quite a while. The Burns's daughter, Janis, had completed three years at the Portland School of Fine and Applied Art and planned to enter the University of Maine. Her favorite subject for sketching, not surprisingly, was seascapes.

William T. Burns died in Castine, Maine, in 1963, at the age of 59.

Howard Beebe (courtesy of Barbara Gaspar)

## Howard B. Beebe
( 1950–1951)

Howard Beebe, born in New London, Connecticut, in 1905, was a veteran of the old Lighthouse Service who joined the U.S. Coast Guard when the Coast Guard took over management of U.S. lighthouses in 1939. His light-keeping career began at New London Ledge Light in Connecticut, where he weathered the infamous hurricane of 1938, which sent waves through the building's second floor. He went on to serve at two light stations on Block Island. After his time at Portland Head, he spent several years at Pomham Rocks Light on the Providence River in Rhode Island.

## Earle E. Benson
(1952–1954)

Earle Benson was born in 1897 in Biddeford, Maine. He served in the U.S. Army in World War I, and later had long career as a lighthouse keeper that began when he became

Wintry view, circa 1954.
U.S. Coast Guard photo.

an assistant keeper at Maine's Great Duck Island Light in the early 1930s. He then became the civilian keeper at Wood Island Light near Biddeford in 1934. When the old Lighthouse Service merged with the U.S. Coast Guard in 1939, Benson joined the Coast Guard and became a chief boatswain's mate. He and his wife, Alice (Descoteaux), were thrilled to get electricity and a television at Wood Island in 1950. Their favorite show was *The Lone Ranger.*

Benson spent the last three years of his career as the Coast Guard officer in charge at Portland Head Light Station. During that period, a woman once walked right into the keeper's house and sat at the kitchen table. The woman insisted that Benson and his wife were government employees, and she demanded service.

Alice Benson later recalled a storm in 1953 that flooded the keeper's house. The glasses in her cabinet weren't broken, she said, but she claimed that each one was filled with water.

Benson retired in 1954 and died in Biddeford at the age of 71 in 1969. Alice was quoted a few years later in *The Salt Book* by Pamela Wood. "It sounds exciting about all these storms that happen and all that kind of stuff goes by," she said of lighthouse life. "That's gone. But you take the other days, you got all them other days to keep goin'. It wasn't so much the exciting things that happen. It's how people live on 'em."

## Archie McLaughlin
### (1956–1957)

Archie McLaughlin was the Coast Guard officer in charge at Portland Head, sharing the light-keeping duties with civilian keeper William T. Burns, an unusual arrangement. McLaughlin, who was from St. George, Maine, lived at the station with his wife and their two daughters, who attended school in South Portland. Before Portland Head, his lighthouse-keeping experience included the Doubling Point Range Lights and Seguin Island.

The McLaughlins' varied hobbies included making decorations from driftwood and searching for Indian relics. "We don't dig scientifically," McLaughlin told a newspaper reporter. "It's a simple way to have fun." Their collection included arrowheads from St. George.

## Henry E. Leonard
### (1957–1960)

Henry Leonard, who was born in Gloucester, Massachusetts, had a long career that began at the Life Saving Station at Popham Beach, Maine, and included about six years of sea duty. During World War II, he served with the U.S. Navy in Iceland, England, and Ireland. He and his wife, Marie, came

Circa 1950s (U.S. Coast Guard photo)

Henry Leonard, right, with Norman W. Zeicke of the Coast Guard at a re-enlistment ceremony (courtesy of the Cape Elizabeth Historical Preservation Society)

to Portland Head in 1957. They had been married for 36 years and had five grandchildren.

## Weston Gamage
(1960–1962)

Wes Gamage, born in Southport, Maine, spent the last part of a 26-year Coast Guard career as the officer in charge at Portland Head Light Station. His wife, Carolyn, said that visitors didn't always respect the posted "open" hours of 9:00 a.m. to 6:00 p.m. The Gamages once tried having a cookout after visiting hours, but the "gallery of curious onlookers" made them feel like they were giving a cooking demonstration, so they gave up on the idea.

The Gamages, who had four children, didn't have time to give tours for all who wanted them, but they did their best to be hospitable. Carolyn always had a pot of coffee ready, and Wes often made doughnuts to offer to tourists. "You probably don't believe it," said Carolyn, "but we sometimes get lonely here."

Circa 1963 (courtesy of the Cape Elizabeth Historical Preservation Society)

## Armand E. Houde
(1962–1965)

Armand Houde was born in Fall River, Massachusetts, in 1927. He served on the *USS Gage* and took part in the Battle of Iwo Jima. He continued in the Coast Guard after World War II and served at several shore stations and on several vessels, including the *Handkerchief Shoal Lightship*, before coming to Portland Head in 1962. He later served as a keeper at Annisquam Light Station in Gloucester, Massachusetts, and retired from the

Coast Guard in 1978. When Houde died in August 2000 in Pompano Beach, Florida, he was survived by his wife, Martha, five sons, three daughters, 23 grandchildren, and four great grandchildren.

## Franklin Allen
(1968–1974)

Franklin "Bob" Allen was originally from Chattanooga, Tennessee, and his wife, Lorraine, was a native Mainer who grew up in Portland. As a girl, Lorraine's family often went to the area around the Two Lights in Cape Elizabeth for family cookouts. Bob and Lorraine met in the late 1950s when Lorraine was working at a drug store and he was on the crew of a Coast Guard cutter.

After two years at Thacher Island off Rockport, Massachusetts, the Allens moved with their four children to Portland Head in 1968. Bob Allen, said his wife, was a man who loved his station. He enjoyed gardening, and

Circa 1973 (from the collection of the author)

(photo by the author)

during the Allen years the grounds had thriving flowerbeds and a carpet of healthy grass.

"Here you really have to watch out for tourists," Lorraine Allen told writer Kim Murphy in 1973. "Your life is not your own, but I love it. The tourists don't bother me, except when they have to use the bathroom. It's mostly older people who do that, and they're always nice and polite."

Once, Lorraine struck up a conversation with a woman artist from Tennessee. The woman wanted to paint the scene in winter, so she was invited back to live for more than a week in a spare room in the keeper's house. Another time, when Lorraine's visiting mother was frying fresh fish in the kitchen and tourists were drooling at the smell, Bob invited a man in to share some of the fish.

A major storm in February 1972 forced Lorraine and the children to evacuate the station. The waves sent rocks, seaweed, and even starfish through a window on the south side of the keeper's house. The storm tore shingles from the roof of the fog signal building, ripped clapboards off the house, and ripped up chunks of the concrete sidewalks around the station.

One day, when the Allens were enjoying a cookout on the lawn outside the keeper's house, a tourist commented, "You don't know how lucky you are to live here." Lorraine answered quickly, "Oh yes I do!"

## Roy Cavanaugh
### (1974–1977)

Roy Cavanaugh, a native of Seattle, Washington, became the officer in charge in August 1974, moving to Portland Head with his wife and three children. His varied Coast Guard experience had already taken him to southern California, Virginia, and Alaska, among other stops.

For a 1975 article in the *Maine Sunday Telegram*, Cavanaugh was asked about the navigational importance

(photo by John Whalen)

of lighthouses in the modern world. "Who's kidding who?" he said. "Today every ship of consequence has radar, sonar, and a whole host of sophisticated electronics equipment. Our service to the big fellow is negligible. It's the little guy who depends on us the most—the hundreds of fishing boats, lobstermen, yachtsmen, and other pleasure boaters who depend upon Portland Head Light for help when needed."

At the time of the article, Cavanaugh and his assistant, Tony Di Nardi, alternated 12-hour shifts (8:00 to 8:00), working days one week and nights the next. They constantly spot-checked 21 buoys in the vicinity; once in a while, a buoy would break loose in a storm. When the Two Lights, four miles to the south, disappeared in the fog, it was time to turn on Portland Head's fog signal.

A frequent visitor during Cavanaugh's stay was Arthur Cameron, son of Keeper John W. Cameron. He enjoyed visits to his childhood home for chats and coffee. "Many of us old-timers here on the cape are very proud of Roy,"

said Cameron. He appreciated the fact that Cavanaugh was working with the Maine Bicentennial Committee to make sure that the lighthouse would play a significant role in the 1976 festivities.

## Raymond Barbar
### (1978–1982)

Raymond Barbar, originally from Sacramento, California, was the officer in charge at the time of a July 1982 article in the *Portland Evening Express*. The constant flow of tourists was simply part of the job, he said. "The lighthouse has a function, but people want to see it. We understand that. By and large we have no trouble," he told the reporter.

Barbar and his assistant, Marion Danna, sent weather data every three hours to Coast Guard Station Portland. Both of the keepers were married with two children, and they lived in opposite sides of the duplex keeper's house.

(photo by the author)

## Michael Cook
(1982–1986)

One of the Coast Guard's last keepers, Michael Cook lived at the station with his wife, Patty, and their two young daughters. When they'd go to the local grocery store, their daughter Jessica—four years old when they left Portland Head—would see a brand of ice cream bars that featured Portland Head Light on the labels, and she'd tell anyone within earshot, "That's my house!"

Cook told a newspaper interviewer that every visitor seemed to have 10,000 questions. "You keep your head down, keep a smile on your face, and keep going straight ahead, otherwise you'd never get any work done in a day," he told a newspaper reporter in 1986. The Cooks often felt like they were living in a fishbowl. One morning, Patty went downstairs in her bathrobe and found two elderly women sitting at the kitchen table. "They wanted to know when breakfast was served," she said.

Another annoyance was the fact that the lighthouse phone number was very similar to that of a local pharmacy. Cook sometimes told callers their prescriptions weren't ready, depending on his mood.

Cook was proud that his daughters got to be part of one of the nation's last lighthouse families. "It will live on in their memories for a long time," he said. "Something to tell the grandkids. Anybody can tell about being an accountant or a truck driver. Not everyone will be able to say, 'I was a lightkeeper.' And soon there won't be any more."

## Nathan Wasserstrom
(1986–1989)

One of the last keepers of Maine's oldest lighthouse, Nathan Wasserstrom lived at Portland Head with his wife, Tina. She echoed some of the previous keepers' comments on visitors: "At times, it's a little like living in a fishbowl. People see the lighthouse

(from the collection of the author)

and think how romantic it all looks, and they'll walk right in the front door while we're eating breakfast. They don't seem to realize this is our home."

When asked if the foghorn bothered him, Wasserstrom would cup his hand over his ear and say, "Huh? What?" as a joke. Their six-year-old son, Kenny, loved the sound of the foghorn so much that he made a recording so he could listen to it on sunny days.

The Wasserstroms' antique pewter lamps grew tarnished from the salt air, and it was impossible to keep the salt off the windows, among other hardships. Still, Tina told a *New York Times* reporter in 1988, "We'll never have another chance to live in a place as wonderful as this."

## Davis Simpson
(1986–1989)

Portland Head's last officer in charge, Davis Simpson, lived at the station with his wife and two young daughters. The kids had to go elsewhere if they wanted to play away from crowds of tourists, and Simpson found the battle to cultivate a nice green lawn to be a losing battle. But they were small prices to pay for the privilege of being one of America's last lighthouse keepers.

Simpson told a United Press reporter in 1989 that he and his family were sad to leave. "It's an experience we're not going to forget, let's put it that way," he said. "The thrill of living in a lighthouse wears off after a while, but something always turns up to make it interesting."

Referring to automation, he commented, "In the long term, they think they're going to save a lot of money, which I think they may very well do. But that's 200 years of history in that tower." At the ceremony on August 7, 1989, Davis Simpson lowered the American flag one last time, and automation took over.

The Liberty Ship *Jeremiah O'Brien*, built nearby at South Portland in 1943, steamed past Portland Head as part of a commemoration of the 50th anniversary of the ship's role in the 1944 D-Day invasion. (courtesy of Don Johnson)

# The Modern Keepers

A lease agreement with the Coast Guard went into effect in 1990, and the Museum at Portland Head Light opened in the renovated keeper's house on July 13, 1992. Present at the opening was Ethel Cameron, daughter-in-law of Keeper John W. Cameron. Also there for the occasion was Frank Purdue, the well-known CEO of one of the largest chicken-producing companies in the United States.

The Museum at Portland Head Light focuses on the history of the lighthouse and Fort Williams. Among the displays are the station's old seven-foot-tall, second-order lens and a fifth-order lens from Maine's Squirrel Point Lighthouse. Near the museum, a garage was converted into a gift shop that features many items that are made in Maine.

Cheryl Parker was the director of the museum for its first decade of existence. In 1992, Parker put an ad in a local paper requesting gardeners who could make the grounds look prettier. The Cape Elizabeth Garden Club stepped in, and volunteers of the club continue to maintain the flower gardens near the lighthouse in the warmer months. Longtime Cape Elizabeth Town Manager Mike McGovern once commented, "Almost as many people get photographed in front of the garden as in front of the lighthouse."

A Cape Elizabeth resident, Jeanne Gross, has been director since 2001. After docent training through Portland Landmarks and time as a volunteer at Spring Point Ledge Light in South Portland, Gross saw the director position at Portland Head as a "dream job."

A Cape Elizabeth Fire Department ladder truck at Portland Head in 2000 (courtesy of the Cape Elizabeth Historical Preservation Society)

In October 1993, the light station property was deeded to the town of Cape Elizabeth. For a few years, part of the keeper's house was rented as an apartment. The first tenants were two Coast Guard ensigns, Matt Stuck and Sam Eisenbeiser. Stuck declared, "There's no other place on this planet with views out of every window." He also said it was strange "seeing pictures of your house everywhere you go."

There was a downside, however. One of the ensigns told reporters, "The disadvantage of living at Portland Head Light is that you're part of the scenery," referring to the constant flow of tourists.

The Portland Headlight at Portland, Maine — D-10

CAPE ELIZABETH, ME. PORTLAND, HEAD LIGHT.

(from the collection of the author)

Glenn Jordan, who lived with his wife in the apartment for the first two years of their marriage, later commented on the experience. "We learned to sleep with a foghorn rattling the bedroom window," he wrote. "We learned why the Head Light could seem like the most crowded and the most isolated place in Maine." Jordan said it was "a pain" to carry a basket of laundry through a crowd of tourists in July, but winter nights were the best. The Jordans left when a daughter, Lily, was born, to give her "room to grow."

Ed Ellis and his wife, Elaine Amass, lived in the apartment for two years. "The view is worth the visitors and the foghorn. If it wasn't, we would have left the first year," said Ed Amass. The former apartment is now used for offices and storage for the museum and gift shop.

Rainbow Construction replaced the deteriorating roof of the keeper's house in 2002, using durable modern red shingles that appear historically authentic. A $260,000 renovation of the lighthouse was completed in the spring of 2005. Some repointing was done on the 80-foot tower, and it was repainted. The keeper's house and gift shop were also painted, and some of the lighthouse's windows were replaced. The lighthouse tower and other buildings were again repaired and repainted in the spring of 2016.

Portland Head Light was one of five New England lighthouses that were featured on a set of U.S. postage stamps

The 2013 New England Coastal Lighthouse forever stamps

The 1981 U.S. postage stamp featuring
Portland Head Light

know, that Portland Head Light is one of the most iconic lighthouses in America," Earle Shettleworth, director of the Maine Historic Preservation Commission, said at the time. A first-day-of-issue event was held at Fort Williams Park on July 13, 2013. It was the second time the lighthouse had been featured on a U.S. postage stamp; the first time was in 1981, when it shared an 18¢ stamp with an American flag and the words "From sea to shining sea."

in 2013, as depicted by artist Howard Koslow. "This affirms what we already

(photo by the author)

# IS IT HAUNTED?

It often seems that lighthouses and ghost stories go together. Portland Head, for such an old station, seems to have few such tales. But Ed Ellis and his wife, Elaine Amass, who lived in the keeper's house for two years, reported that their motion-sensor alarm on the stairs sometimes went off at night when nobody—at least nobody they could see—was there. And Geraldine Reed, who lived in the keeper's house with her husband, Coast Guardsman Tom Reed, in the 1960s, wrote in *Lighthouse Digest* that she believed there was a ghost in residence. The only place she felt the presence of the ghost was in the basement of the keeper's house. "My feeling is that he was a friendly ghost and just needed to be told that his keeper days were over and he could rest in peace," she wrote.

David Wells, psychic medium from the TV show *Most Haunted*, at the lighthouse in 2008 (photo by the author)

Glenn Jordan, who later lived in the apartment in the keeper's house, said that he once saw a "scruffy" man in "blue sailor's attire" scowling at him through a window. Perhaps the oddest thing was that he went back to the same spot a few minutes later, and not only was there no man outside the window, but there was no window in that part of the house.

In August 2008, a "Haunted Lighthouses Bus Tour" visited Portland Head. The group included Ron Kolek, paranormal investigator for New England Ghost Project, and several prominent psychic mediums. David Wells, an English medium best known for the TV show *Most Haunted*, said he felt the presence in the keeper's house of a little girl, seven or eight years old, named Mary. Wells felt that the girl's spirit was happy and laughing. Another person on the same tour, Maureen Wood, a medium who has worked with New England Ghost Project, felt the strong presence of a past lighthouse keeper in the museum area of the house, and she sensed a great sadness about him. She felt that the man had to retire because of heart trouble, and she "heard" him repeat a particular phrase over and over: "I gave my life to the light."

The second-order Fresnel lens was replaced by a rotating DCB-36 aerobeacon in 1958, raising the power of the light from 30,000 to 200,000 candlepower. For many years, the old lens was kept in storage at the Mystic Seaport Museum in Connecticut. When the Museum at Portland Head

The second-order Fresnel lens that was once used in the lighthouse is one of the centerpieces of the Museum at Portland Head Light. (photo by the author)

Lighthouse opened, the lens was loaned for display. Due to space limitations, only half of the lens is displayed.

The lighthouse now has a rotating DCB-224 aerobeacon exhibiting a white flash every four seconds, 101 feet above mean high water, 24 hours a day. The light remains an active aid to navigation, as does the fog signal. The fog signal was converted to a new "mariner-activated" system in 2016, meaning mariners can turn it on with a VHF radio.

Looking up at the DCB-224 optic (photo by the author)

(photo by the author)

# WHAT'S THAT OTHER LIGHTHOUSE OUT THERE?

Look out into Casco Bay, east of Portland Head Light, and you'll see a weather-worn granite lighthouse on a rocky ledge, a little over a mile away. That is Ram Island Ledge Light, 90 feet tall, built in 1905. Keepers lived inside the tower until 1959, when the light was automated. Joe Johansen, a Coast Guard keeper at Ram Island Ledge around 1949–1950, later said: "You could have been living in the 1800s because, other than the link with the radio, there were no conveniences at all. Nothing. It was lonesome in a way, but you were never really lonely, because there were always two of you aboard. In the winters the nights were kind of long because you split the watch . . . You usually stood watch in the galley because that's where your only source of heat was: a kerosene stove, which we used for cooking and heat."

In 2010, Ram Island Ledge Light was sold via online auction to Dr. Jeffrey Florman of Windham, Maine, for $190,000.

Way out in Casco Bay, on a clear day, you can also see Halfway Rock Light about nine miles away. Halfway Rock Light is another wave-swept granite tower, built in 1871. And on certain very clear days, you can see all the way to Seguin Light, some 23 miles away. This is possible because the lighthouse on Seguin Island is Maine's highest above the ocean, with a focal plane height of 186 feet.

Look to south from Portland Head and you can spot the Two Lights of Cape Elizabeth about four miles away—the active east light is to the left and the inactive west light is above the tree line to the right. And look in the opposite direction, to the north toward South Portland and Portland, and you will see Spring Point Ledge Light a little over two miles distant.

That make seven lighthouses you can see from Portland Head in clear weather, including Portland Head Light itself. There are few locations that can rival this impressive total.

From left to right: Ram Island Ledge Light, Halfway Rock Light, Seguin Light, Spring Point Ledge Light, and the east light of the Two Lights in Cape Elizabeth (all photos by the author)

# THE GODDARD MANSION

As you drive into Fort Williams Park, look uphill to the left through the trees, and you will see the remains of the once-spectacular Goddard Mansion. The Victorian house with Italianate touches was designed by the noted New York architect Charles A. Alexander for local businessman and Civil War veteran John Goddard (1811–1870). Goddard made his fortune in the lumber business and purchased the Cape Cottage, a popular resort hotel.

Completed in 1859, the mansion was sold in 1898 to Judge Joseph W. Symonds. With the expansion of Fort Williams around 1900, the mansion was acquired by the military and was converted to quarters for noncommissioned officers. The basement was the noncommissioned officers' club.

When the Town of Cape Elizabeth purchased Fort Williams in 1964, the mansion was in poor condition. By 1981, it was considered a nuisance, and the town manager recommended that it be razed. After some debate, a compromise was reached. The fire department burned the interior to remove dangerous debris, but the outer walls were left standing. Fencing around the building was added in 2009 due to safety concerns.

The remains of the Goddard Mansion
(photo by the author)

During the 2016 repainting (photo by the author)

Coast Guard aids to navigation personnel from Station South Portland maintain the navigational equipment, but the town maintains the remainder of the property. A $65,000 repainting project of the lighthouse tower was completed in the spring of 2016.

The Museum at Portland Head Light, a crown jewel of the New England coast, has welcomed visitors from every state in the United States and over 75 countries. For more information on the lighthouse and museum, contact The Museum at Portland Head Light, 1000 Shore Road, Cape Elizabeth, ME 04107. Phone: (207) 799-2661. Web site: www. portlandheadlight.com.

(photo by the author)

NEW YORK STEAMER PASSING PORTLAND HEAD LIGHT 80

PRESS HERALD — EXPRESS PHOTO

12.539

(from the collection of the author)

(photo by the author)

# Selected Bibliography

Bachelder, Peter Dow. *Lighthouses of Casco Bay*. Portland, Maine: Breakwater Press, 1975.

Caldwell, Bill. *Lighthouses of Maine*. Portland, Maine: Gannett Books, 1986.

Cape Elizabeth Historical Preservation Society. *Cape Elizabeth Past to Present*. Cape Elizabeth, Maine: Town of Cape Elizabeth, 1991.

Clifford, J. Candace, and Mary Louise Clifford. *Maine Lighthouses: Documentation of Their Past*. Alexandria, Virginia: Cypress Communications, 2005.

*Collections from Cape Elizabeth, Maine*. Town of Cape Elizabeth, 1965.

D'Entremont, Jeremy. *The Lighthouses of Maine*. Beverly, Massachusetts: Commonwealth Editions, 2009.

D'Entremont, Jeremy. *The Lighthouses of Maine: Southern Maine to Casco Bay*. Carlisle, Massachusetts: Commonwealth Editions, an imprint of Applewood Books, 2013.

Edwards, George Thornton. *The Youthful Haunts of Longfellow*. Portland, Maine: Published by the author, 1907.

Elwell, Edward H. *Elwell's Portland and Vicinity*. Portland, Maine: Greater Portland Landmarks, Inc., 1975.

Fogg, C. Newhall. "First Light on United States Coast." *Lewiston Journal Magazine*, October 12–15, 1910.

Harrison, Timothy. *Portland Head Light: A Pictorial Journey Through Time*. Wells, ME: Foghorn Publishing, 2006.

Heffernan, John Paul. "Wreck of a China Clipper." *Down East*, January 1964.

Holland, Francis Ross, Jr. *America's Lighthouses: An Illustrated History*. New York, New York: Dover Publications, Inc., 1972.

Jordan, William B. *A History of Cape Elizabeth, Maine*. Bowie, Maryland: Heritage Books, Inc., 1987 (facsimile reprint edition). Originally published 1965.

Mathan, Christiane and William D. Barry. "Portland Head Lighthouse." *The Keeper's Log*, U.S. Lighthouse Society, summer 1991.

Rummler, Kathleen G. *Portland Head Light: Maine's Oldest Lighthouse*. Cape Elizabeth, Maine: The Museum at Portland Head Light, 1997.

Snow, Edward Rowe. *The Lighthouses of New England*. New York, New York: Dodd, Mead & Company, 1973.

Snow, Edward Rowe. *The Romance of Casco Bay*. New York, New York: Dodd, Mead & Company, 1975.

Sterling, Robert Thayer. *Lighthouses of the Maine Coast and the Men Who Keep Them*. Brattleboro, Vermont: Stephen Daye Press, 1935.

Strout, John. "A Strout Family Tradition." *Lighthouse Digest*, May 1997.

Thompson, Kenneth E., Jr. *Portland Head Light and Fort Williams*. Portland, Maine: The Thompson Group, 1998.

Thomson, William O. *Portland Head Light: A Place in History*. Kennebunk, Maine: 'Scapes Me, 2004.

Willoughby, Malcolm F. *Lighthouses of New England*. Boston, Massachusetts: T.O. Metcalf Company, 1929.

## ONLINE SOURCES

Ancestry.com, Newspapers.com, Newspaperarchive.com, Genealogybank.com, *Boston Globe* archives

New England Lighthouses: A Virtual Guide – www.newenglandlighthouses.net

Lighthouse Friends – www.lighthousefriends.com

# About the Author

Jeremy D'Entremont has been involved with lighthouses for more than three decades. He has written more than a dozen books (including *The Lighthouse Handbook: New England, The Lighthouse Handbook: West Coast, and All About Nubble Light*) and hundreds of articles on lighthouses and other maritime subjects. His photographs have appeared in countless books and magazines. He is the historian for the American Lighthouse Foundation and founder of Friends of Portsmouth Harbor Lighthouses. He has appeared on national TV and radio and has lectured on his favorite subject from Maine to California. Jeremy lives in Portsmouth, New Hampshire, with his wife, Charlotte Raczkowski, and their tuxedo cat, Evie.

On September 18, 2010, Jeremy D'Entremont spoke at Portland Head Light during the opening ceremony for Maine Open Lighthouse Day. (photo by William Marshall)

# About Cider Mill Press
# Book Publishers

Good ideas ripen with time. From seed to harvest, Cider Mill Press brings fine reading, information, and entertainment together between the covers of its creatively crafted books. Our Cider Mill bears fruit twice a year, publishing a new crop of titles each spring and fall.

*"Where Good Books Are Ready for Press"*

Visit us online at
cidermillpress.com

or write to us at
PO Box 454
12 Spring St.
Kennebunkport, Maine 04046